Contents

Director's Foreword

Agreeing on what makes a great portrait is a matter of intense debate, particularly when starting with over 5,000 photographs submitted from around the world to be judged anonymously. The process is made more complex – although also more fascinating – by the range of genres and types of portraits submitted: here is a beautifully arranged subject in the home, here a person captured in the street and there an artfully lit studio portrait. The 2006 Photographic Portrait Prize judges understood the terms of the debate extremely well, but they were ready to review the issues as required, considering technical expertise, context information – from the background of an image to the title of the portrait itself – and the all-encompassing matter of human presence and engagement. In the final stages of selecting the photographs to be included in the exhibition and those to be shortlisted for a prize, the judges frequently came back to the simple proposition of whether we had been introduced to a new person. In every instance it seemed to me that we had – and with tremendous skill and conviction – and that we could legitimately ask how much we should know of their character and life.

The number and variety of entries once again demonstrated the liveliness of photographic portraiture as a genre of interest to photographers of all ages and generations. I should very much like to thank all the photographers who submitted their work: the exhibition depends entirely on their discrimination and determination. I offer my congratulations to the winners, Richard Boll, Anna Bauer, Kiran Master and Kyoto Hamada. I offer additional congratulations to Erin Kornfeld, the winner of The Deloitte Commission for 2006, awarded to a photographer aged twenty-five or younger. We are very grateful for Deloitte's exceptional support for contemporary photographic portraiture at the National Portrait Gallery over recent years.

I would like to thank my fellow judges: David Chandler, Jenny Dyson, Grace Lau and Terence Pepper. They were unstinting in their concentration and appropriately robust in their discussions and debates. My thanks also go to the staff at the National Portrait Gallery, particularly Joanna Banham, Pim Baxter, Caroline Brooke Johnson, Naomi Conway, Denise Ellitson, Neil Evans, Clare Freestone, Ruth Müller-Wirth, Jonathan Rowbotham, Sarah Tinsley, Rosie Wilson and especially Sue Thompson, as well as the designers NB: Studio and the interviewer Richard McClure, for all their hard work on organizing the submission, the selection process, the exhibition and this catalogue.

Schweppes sponsored the Photographic Portrait Prize from 2003–05 and we are now seeking a title sponsor for 2007 onwards.

Sandy Nairne, Director,
National Portrait Gallery

Judging the Competition

What makes a winning portrait? As one of the judges for this year's Photographic Portrait Prize, I asked myself this question 5,000 times as each entry was carefully considered. Having worked in fashion magazines for the last ten years, I found the judging to be a more intense version of what is one of the most exciting aspects of my job. As the European editor of a teenage magazine, I am always looking out for photographers who can capture the youthfulness of teen spirit in a fresh, wholesome way. The photography is bright, upbeat and fun with the emphasis on capturing something beautiful and joyful in the subjects. It's a technicolour, celebratory spin on what it is to be a fashionable teen today.

With this in mind, I was particularly intrigued by the images of teenagers submitted to this year's Photographic Portrait Prize. Teenage youth cannot help but be fascinating and beguiling. One such image by John Nassari (above right – see p.42) lingered in my mind as a brilliant metaphor for that moment between being a child and being a grown-up. A girl, aged around sixteen, stands in the doorway holding an unlit cigarette. Usually I loathe cigarettes as props to a portrait but somehow the unlit aspect made me question if this girl was playing at smoking. Framed by the doorway, I see her badly applied lip liner and body-hugging top and it all looks so ambiguous. Is she a young mum-to-be? Is she pretending? Is it fancy dress? What is going on behind her? There is something so knowing about the girl, yet through her gaze, the photographer has captured fragility. Here is a teenager proudly confronting the viewer, yet she is awkward about her body and is doing her best to conceal that awkwardness via her wardrobe choices and that cocky 'yeah, what?' look that British teens do with such aplomb. A real winner.

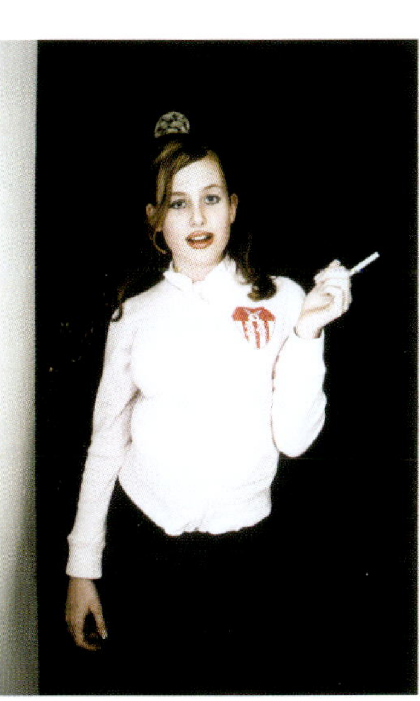

Having launched *Rubbish* magazine earlier this year, a hardback fashion annual that celebrates the silly side of style, I was also intrigued by any portraits that played with humour in an original way. Noted for its humour among the entries was a fantastic portrait of a father and his daughter by Michiru Nakayamam (below right – see p.50). Dressed identically, they are sitting in the same position and facing the same direction on a sofa with violins on their knees. Strictly, this is not a fashion image. But in the context of what I am always looking out for, I loved it. Do they play in an orchestra together? Is dressing alike in their DNA? Aside from being a quirky spin on a family portrait, it was one of the few images that made me smile. And why not?

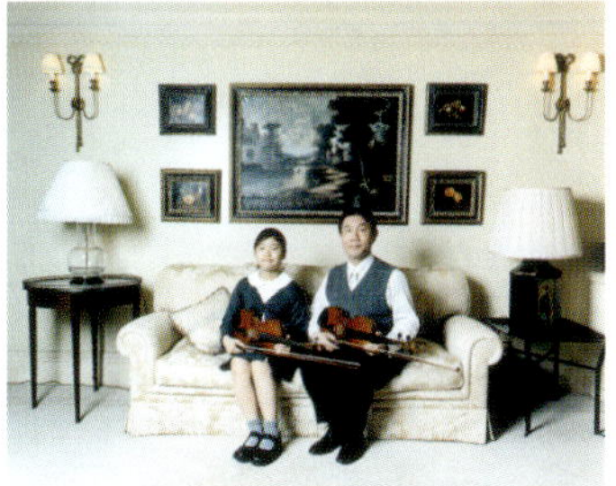

Jenny Dyson, European Editor, *Teen Vogue* and Editor-in-Chief, *Rubbish* magazine
www.rubbishmag.com

The Prizes

Photographic Portrait Prize
The Photographic Portrait Prize is open to photographers from around the world aged eighteen or over.

The first prize winner is Richard Boll, who receives £12,000.

The second prize winner is Anna Bauer, who receives £1,500.

The third prize winner is Kiran Master, who receives £1,000.

The fourth prize winner is Hamada Kyoko, who receives £500.

The Deloitte Commission
The Deloitte Commission is for the best portrait taken by a photographer aged twenty-five or under.

The winner is Erin Kornfeld, who receives £5,000.

If you would like to join the mailing list to receive an ontry form for next year's Photographic Portrait Prize, please send your full contact details to:

Photographic Portrait Prize 2007 Marketing Department National Portrait Gallery St Martin's Place London WC2H 0HE

The Judges

Chair: Sandy Nairne, Director, National Portrait Gallery
The 2006 entries for the Photographic Portrait Prize were of a very high standard. From around the world, photographers of all ages and backgrounds had submitted the portraits of people that really mattered to them: there was a sense of conviction and commitment. As always, it was fascinating coming to a common view of the best images and there were many more that were in close contention to be included in the shortlist. I am sure the debate will continue in the exhibition itself.

David Chandler
Director, Photoworks
The volume of photographs was immediately intimidating. How can four portraits be chosen from thousands? And all in two days! Thankfully, the National Portrait Gallery has a well-drilled system that eases the selection process without compromising it. But because the competition attracts so many remarkable photographs decisions become increasingly difficult to make.

Having to concentrate so hard on such a wide variety of work has some very positive effects. It forces you to seriously reconsider what makes a good portrait, and it also means that your judgement is continually put to the test. Another more unpredictable effect of this intensive process is that, for a while at least, you begin to see the world as a steady stream of possible portraits drifting in and out of view. It reminded me how much the ebb and flow of our lives is conditioned by the people we come into contact with, whether they be family, friends or complete strangers. Part of the value of photographic portraits is that they make us realize that inside our routine everyday experiences the ordinary is often extraordinary.

Jenny Dyson, European Editor, *Teen Vogue* and Editor-in-Chief, *Rubbish* magazine
It was a huge honour to be invited to judge such an important photography prize and the calibre of submissions was astounding. The process was the aesthetic equivalent of a marathon as we were looking at on average 100 images every half hour!

I was intrigued by how instinctive the reactions of all of us were when an entry truly was visually arresting. There was equal confidence from the panel over the portraits that didn't quite move us enough to want to keep them in the final selection. I had no idea how emotional the process would become for me. My two favourite images were so powerful that I am still recalling further nuances from each of them, which I hadn't during the final decision-making moments. And to me that is the essence of a great portrait: something that stays with you, imprinted into your mind – evocative, stirring and true.

Grace Lau, Photographer, Writer and Lecturer
It was an awesome experience: to evaluate over 5,000 portraits in just two intensive days involves the highest power of concentration, an objective analytical mind and excellent eyesight, not to mention a lot of stamina.

The diversity of submissions was incredibly exciting and I was pleased to see the return of black-and-white portraits, but disappointed that so many were poorly printed in muddy grey. I also despaired to see so many stereotypical images flash by: holiday shots of wrinkled old men and dirty ragged kids within an exotic environment. Babies in baths and couples on couches were other favourites, and unless these were visually exceptional or expressed some profound or critical comment, they were generally rejected.

Although the standard of work was generally high, I wanted to see fewer literal representations and more creative interpretations. But it was so brilliant to experience the history of photography in the making: this annual National Portrait Gallery event is so important that it is shaping the direction of the genre of photographic portraiture.

Terence Pepper, Curator of Photographs, National Portrait Gallery
The entries for 2006 maintained the high quality of previous years. It would have been possible to create an equally enthralling exhibition with sixty other finalists. Predicting the finalists continues to be a mysterious and inexplicable conundrum. Although the judges found consensus on a number of images this year, what most struck this judge were the individual pictures each person championed that didn't overlap with anyone else's opinion. For this reason the final selection represents many differing but fascinating views that justify a group approach.

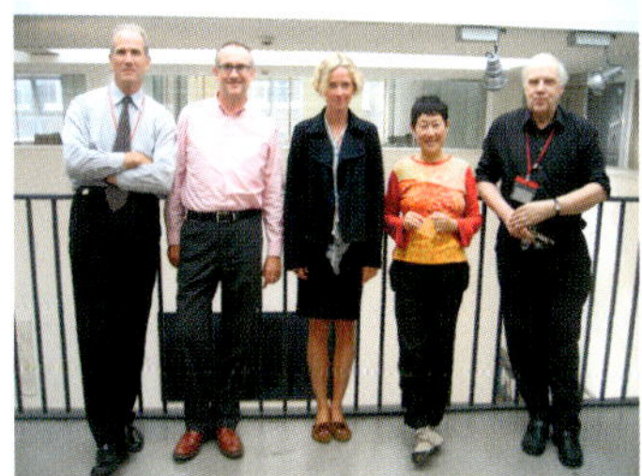

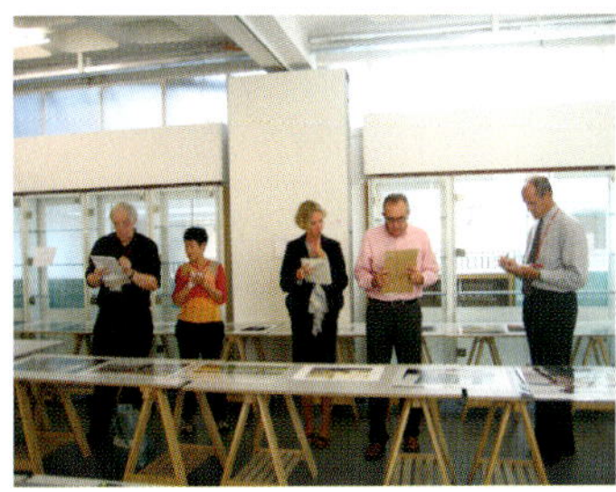

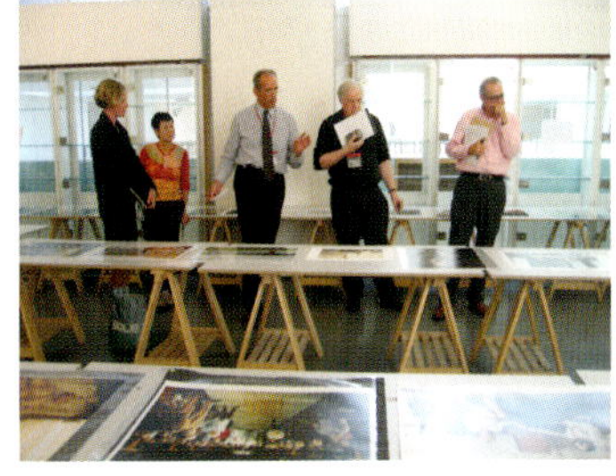

First Prize Winner Richard Boll

Born in Kenya but brought up on the Isle of Wight, Richard Boll began taking photographs as a teenager, experimenting at first with black-and-whites of the local landscape. What started out as a pastime quickly became an addiction. 'Photography became both a hobby and an obsessive-compulsive disorder,' he explains. 'I was determined to create a life for myself in which I could perpetually take and deal with pictures.'

Towards that goal, Boll took a BA in Photography at Edinburgh College of Art, graduating in 1999. He remained at the college in a teaching capacity for the next five years until a growing demand from the advertising industry gave him sufficient confidence to set up full-time as a commercial photographer. 'While taking my degree I'd realized pretty soon that my blurred seascapes and pictures of drying socks weren't going to keep me in gin and dog food for very long,' says Boll, now twenty-nine. 'I had to figure out how to make photography pay.'

Inspired by photographers such as Irving Penn and Nadav Kander who juggle art and commerce, Boll now specializes in still-life and architectural client-work while also pursuing his own personal projects. In 2004, he won the Audi/Next Level Contemporary Photography Award for his minimalist images of artists' studios. Since relocating to Brighton earlier this year, he has worked on Pavement, a series of 'very informal, quickly shot' portraits of passers-by. 'Brighton has a very diverse population – that's why I enjoy taking portraits there. If I can't take a decent portrait in Brighton, I can't take one anywhere.'

Taken from his Pavement series, Boll's winning entry, *Joe*, was shot outside his flat with a Canon 1 Ds Mk II, plus on-camera flash in order to control the exposure of the subject whilst over-exposing the background and throwing it out of focus. 'Joe immediately interested me. It was a quick encounter, three or four minutes, most of which was spent persuading him to pose. Joe insisted he wasn't photogenic. I disagreed. With this kind of portraiture, there's a level of trust that has to be won in a short space of time, and I always tell my subjects to be themselves. It lets them know I'm not out to misrepresent them; that I'm not being unkind.

'In Joe's portrait there are some details that hint at a certain level of vulnerability, but these are played off against other details, like his tattoos and adornments, that suggest a real resilience and self-belief. His expression is quite complex and defies interpretation. I didn't appreciate the significance of having the cars in the background until I was looking at the image later. I now feel they really hold the portrait together.'

Interviewed by
Richard McClure

Richard Boll **Joe**
from the series
Pavement
June 2006

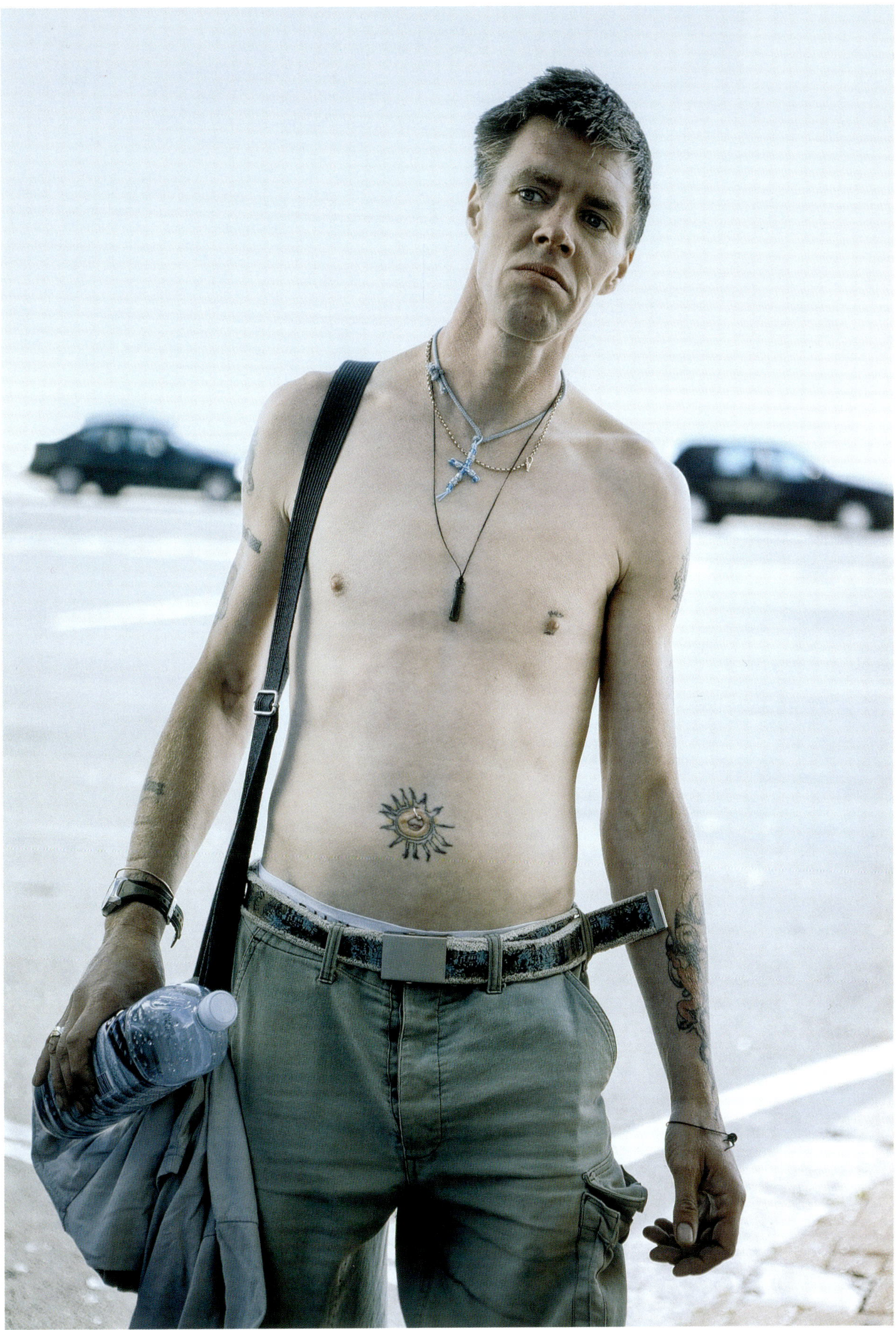

Second Prize Winner
Anna Bauer

Although Anna Bauer admits that her world was 'shattered' when her parents divorced during her childhood, the thirty-year-old photographer rejects any suggestion that her family portraiture represents a bid to reconnect with her past. Based in New York, Bauer regularly returns to her native Germany to photograph her half-siblings and other family members for a series Them, Growing. Her portrait *Jungs, Living Room, Schönstadt* shows her twelve-year-old half-brother Henry and his friends 'waiting to get access to the TV' during a long weekend.

'There is a psychological motivation behind the series, but it's not any cheesy notion of rebuilding my own childhood,' says Bauer, who shot the portrait with a large-format 4x5 camera. 'I don't remember parts of my childhood, so it is more a fascination with that rich part of life. I photograph my half-brothers simply because I'm interested in experiencing their way of seeing and doing. Since I don't live with them, I view them almost like a visitor. Through this project I almost become one of them; they allow me to join their world.'

With her sister set to give birth, Bauer intends to continue the project over the coming years, creating an intimate family narrative in the manner of US photographer Lee Friedlander, who has documented his home life for the past half-century. 'In terms of style, Friedlander is not an influence, but I love his book *Family*. There is a strong personality and authenticity behind his pictures, a very clear voice and I'm drawn to that. Like him, I take a lot of self-portraits, often when something important has happened, or when I'm staying in a hotel room while travelling. It's a way of keeping track of myself.'

Leaving Germany for the US in 2002, Bauer gained a BFA (Batchelor of Fine Arts) in Photography from the School of Visual Arts in New York, and now combines editorial assignments for a variety of magazines with assisting work for several photographers. She has exhibited in several group shows, and twice been featured in the world-touring Festival of Emerging Photographers.

Most recently she has completed a series of triptychs portraying people in their eighties who still work in their professions, be it blacksmith, sculptor or radio presenter. 'I thought it was fascinating to see how their jobs became part of their body, and also to show the continuity of their work over so many decades. In my portraits, whether of family or others, I want people to reveal something of themselves. It's important for me to show a real connection between me and the sitters.'

Interviewed by
Richard McClure

Anna Bauer

Jungs,
Living Room,
Schönstadt
from the series
Them, Growing
May 2005

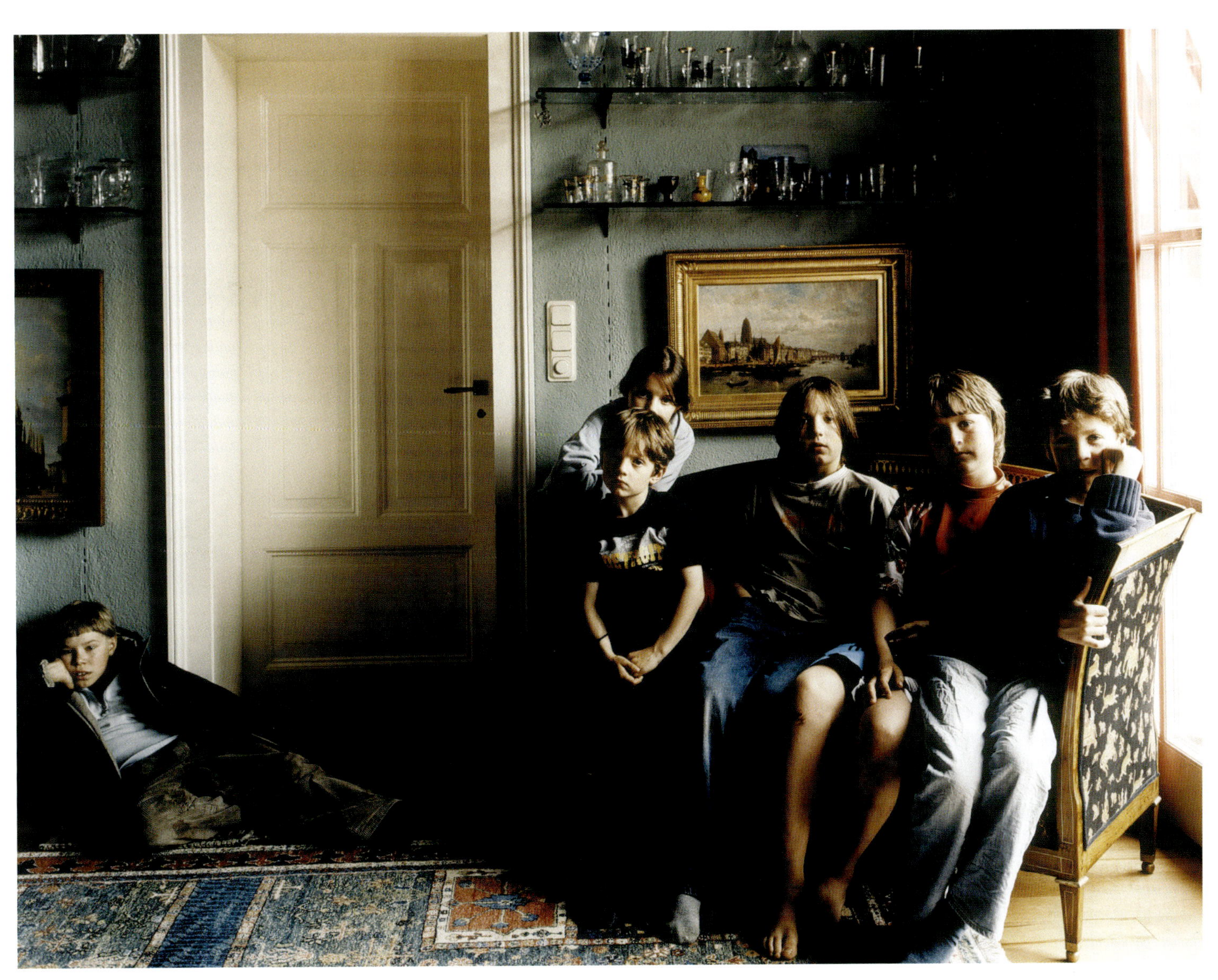

Third Prize Winner Kiran Master

A degree in film, photographic and video arts from the Polytechnic of Central London (now the University of Westminster) pointed him in the right direction, followed by a two-year spell assisting. Since setting up his own studio in 1992, he has become one of the UK's leading commercial photographers. Campaigns for clients such as Microsoft, Virgin, Ford and Mercedes have landed him the industry's top prizes, including a clutch of AOP (Association of Photographers) awards and two Golden Lions from the International Advertising Festival in Cannes. 'I end up shooting a lot in suburbia,' he smiles. 'Clients know not to come to me if they want a car whizzing round a glamorous location.'

Although he has yet to exhibit, Master is beginning to focus more on personal projects, recently returning from a trip to northern Russia where he photographed 'Stalinist concrete blocks' surrounded by desolate wilderness. 'Some landscapes are heavy with a sense of emptiness, and I seek them out all over the place,' he says. 'But I don't just want to create bleak pictures. In the photograph of Michelle, the environment looks distant and cold, but I hope her presence also conveys a strong sense of life, albeit contained and confined.'

Interviewed by
Richard McClure

Ostensibly a portrait of actress and model Michelle Connolly, Kiran Master's untitled entry is not so much a conventional character study as an artistic expression of the photographer's long-held interest in themes of emptiness and isolation. After months spent scouting for a location that communicated a 'sense of absence', Master shot the picture with a 5x4 Linhof Technikarden at an educational training centre in London, casting Connolly as a character in a carefully created scene.

'The portrait isn't about Michelle, she's just one element in the image,' he explains. 'The photograph is more an expression of my conscious or subconscious preoccupations. Isolation runs through a lot of my images, emerging possibly from a strong sense of disconnection between our lives and the environments we create for ourselves.'

Brought up in the 'suburban sprawl' of Pinner by an Indian father and English mother, Master believes his own childhood environment deeply informs his work. 'My parents were very isolated in suburbia – my mother because she was an artist, my father because of his skin colour. I was an introverted, awkward child and I suppose that sense of being an outsider is still deeply ingrained.'

Aged forty-six, Master originally took a degree in politics and international relations, but was swayed from his chosen career path when a friend showed him several pictures he had taken of icicles. 'I finally woke up,' he recalls. 'I promptly went and got a job selling aerial photographs. It took six months for me to realize that this was not my passport to the world of photography.'

Kiran Master **Untitled**
April 2005

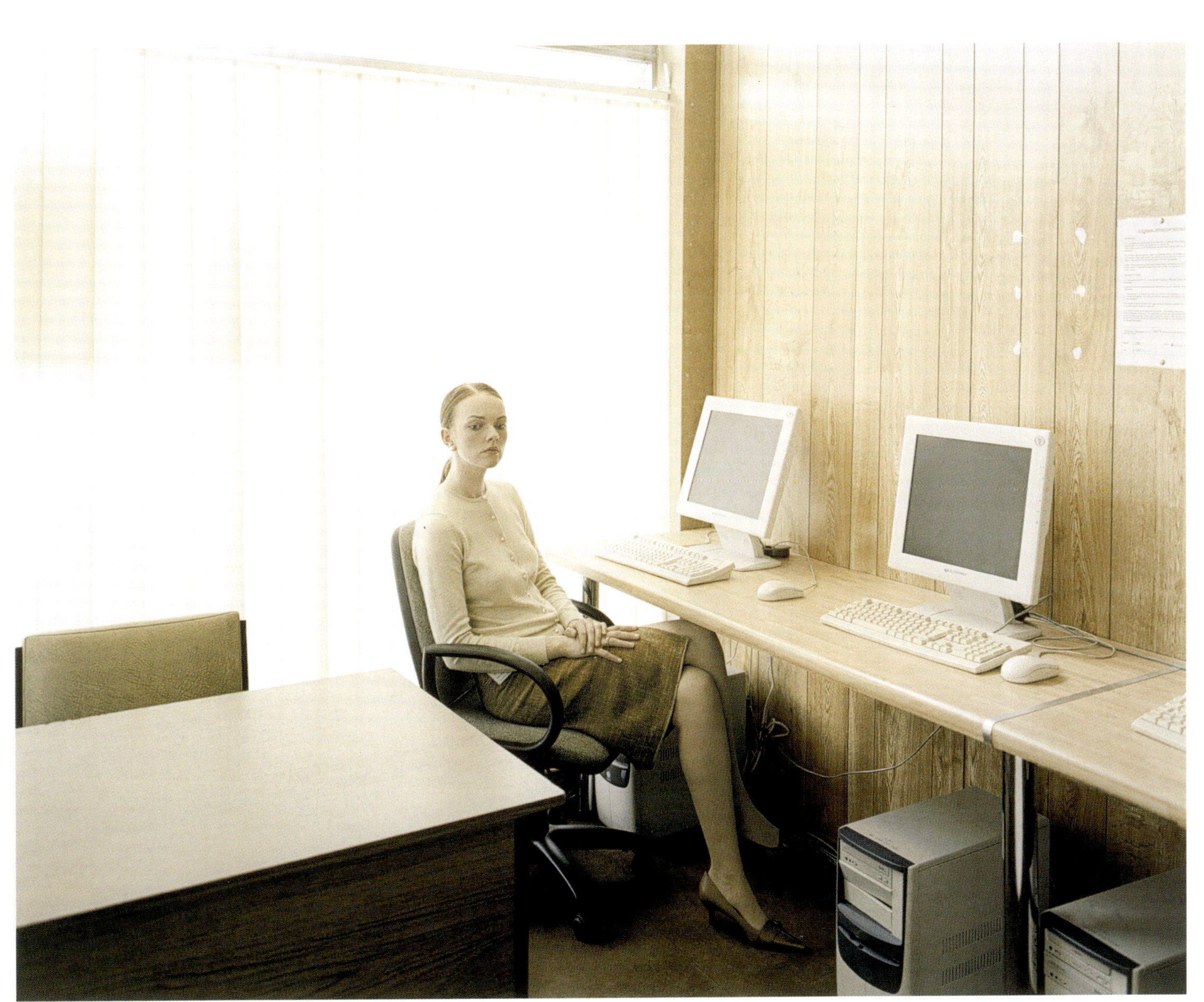

Fourth Prize Winner Kyoko Hamada

Moving to small-town West Virginia with her Japanese parents at the age of fifteen, Tokyo-born Kyoko Hamada spoke no English for several years following her arrival in the US, an inability which she believes led to her interest in the visual arts. 'I spent a good few years without speaking or understanding English, and ended up just looking curiously at what was happening around me,' she explains. 'Maybe I became more observant because of that experience. I was able to tell a lot about people simply by watching their mannerisms and gestures.'

After studying art history and fine art painting in New York, Hamada switched to photography, initially taking pictures of 'simple things like a chicken bone in the snow'. Now aged thirty-three and living in Brooklyn, she has worked as a photographer for the past six years, combining big-budget advertising campaigns for the likes of Microsoft with prize-winning editorial work for the *New York Times*, *Washington Post*, *Fortune* and *Entertainment Weekly*. Earlier this year, her images were included in a group show, Eleven, at the Michael Hoppen Gallery in London.

Hamada's style is in part influenced by British Pop Art, in particular David Hockney's use of colour and composition. 'His use of space seems so simple on the surface, but it is actually rather organized. There's quirkiness and a sense of humour in his art too. Likewise, a lot of my photographs are intended to cause a quiet chuckle.'

Taken with a Mamiya RZ, with tripod and hand-held flash, her fourth-placed entry, *Emily and her Grandmother,* is one of a series of pictures shot on the shores of Lake Placid in upstate New York. Hamada came across the pair accidentally while they were rehearsing a song to perform at a family celebration.

'Emily was practising a song for her sister's wedding, but I like the fact that the viewer has no idea why she is singing by a lake, nor what song she is performing,' says Hamada. 'For me, photography is most interesting when it doesn't fully explain itself and leaves enough room for the viewer to wonder, and imagine the story.

'I like portraits that trigger other thoughts or meaning, beyond being a document of that specific person. Photography works best when the very ordinary and everyday is turned into something else, so I layer my own fantasies onto the real existing people or situations. If my photographs sometimes look strange and surreal, that's because life can often be strange and surreal.'

Interviewed by
Richard McClure

Kyoko Hamada Emily and her Grandmother *from the series* Hometown April 2005

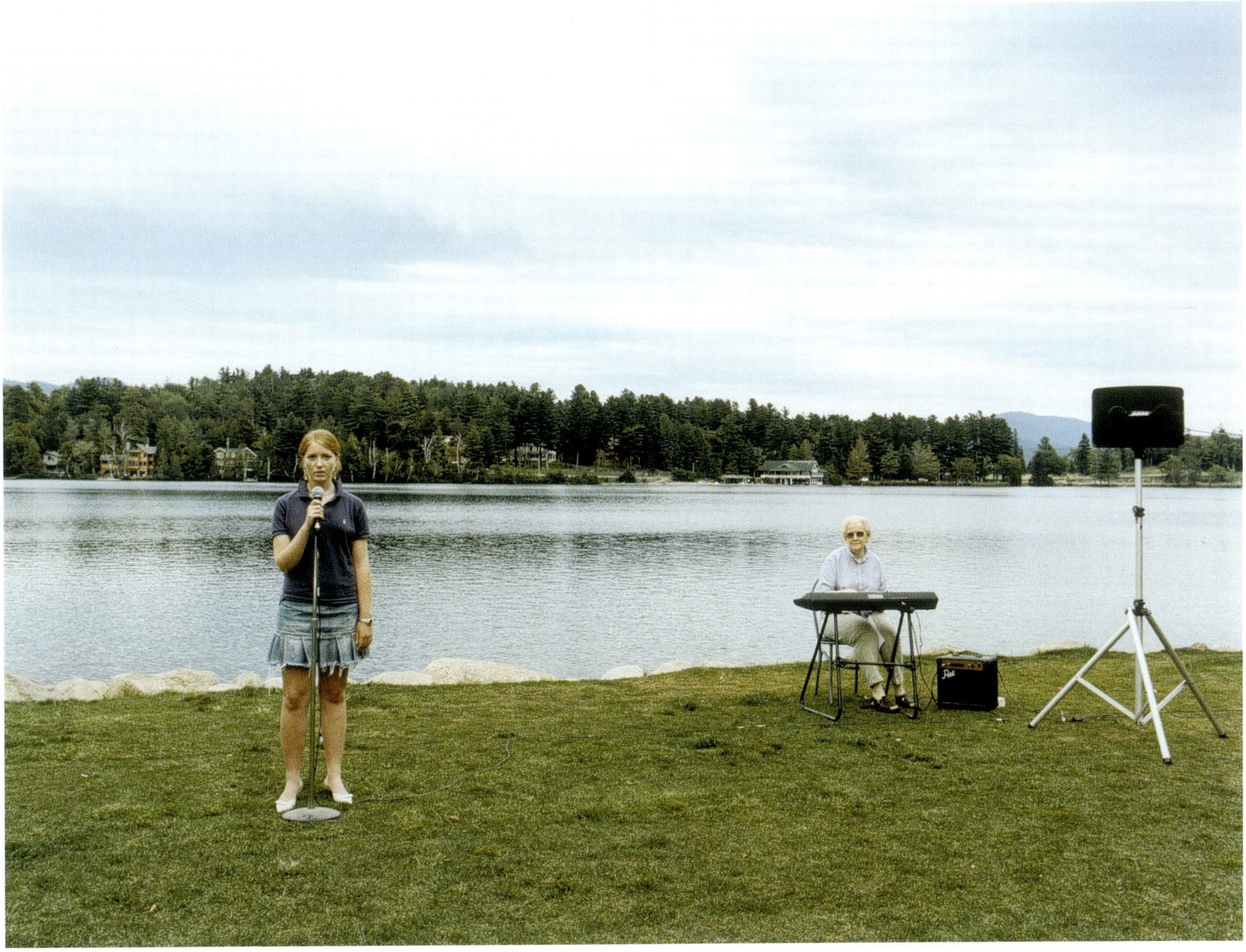

The Deloitte Commission Winner
Erin Kornfeld

The winner of The Deloitte Commission receives a cash prize as well as the opportunity to undertake a portrait commission for Deloitte and the National Portrait Gallery.

Winner of The Deloitte Commission for best portrait taken by a photographer aged twenty-five or under, Erin Kornfeld was born in Greensboro, North Carolina. Aged twenty-four, she discovered the camera's 'magical qualities' as a teenager while taking a class with US photographer Shelby Lee Adams, best known for his portraits of mountain backwoods families in the Appalachia region of Kentucky.

'Shelby's mission is not to belittle his subjects, who suffer huge economic hardships, but to dignify their lives through an honest, loving eye,' explains Kornfeld. 'Seeing his work, I realized the camera's ability to empower people. I also wanted to make people feel confident, powerful and unique through the experience of documenting their essence.'

Using the camera as a near-mystical tool 'to communicate on a deeper level' with her subjects, Kornfeld mostly photographs family and friends. Her winning portrait, *Prudence and Julie*, depicts two of her closest friends one Sunday morning at their home in Tivoli, a small town on the Hudson River. Using a Mamiya 6x7, she lit the scene with a small flash tilted at the ceiling.

'I've photographed Prudence and Julie many times before. We were reading the news and drinking coffee, trying to piece together the remnants of the night before. I wanted to capture their relaxed state in the serenity of the Sunday morning light. Locations are very important to me. I like to get to know people by photographing them in environments that reflect who they are. The environment reveals a sense of place and history that represents the nature of the individual.'

After gaining a BA in Photography from Bard College in Annandale-on-Hudson, New York, where she studied under Stephen Shore and Larry Fink, Kornfeld moved to London in 2005 and recently finished an MA in Art Business at Sotheby's Institute of Art. During her time in the UK, she has established the East London Art Company, a non-profit organization that helps community artists, and braved the less high-minded side of the business by assisting on shoots for *FHM* magazine.

Following her success in the Photographic Portrait Prize, Kornfeld intends to move back to the US and set up her own studio. 'I've wanted to be a freelance photographer ever since I saw my first image appear in the developer,' she says. 'I want to explore all possibilities and use the camera to express my thoughts. For me, photography is a personal search. I want to uncover unknown mysteries – and I want to share these discoveries with others.'

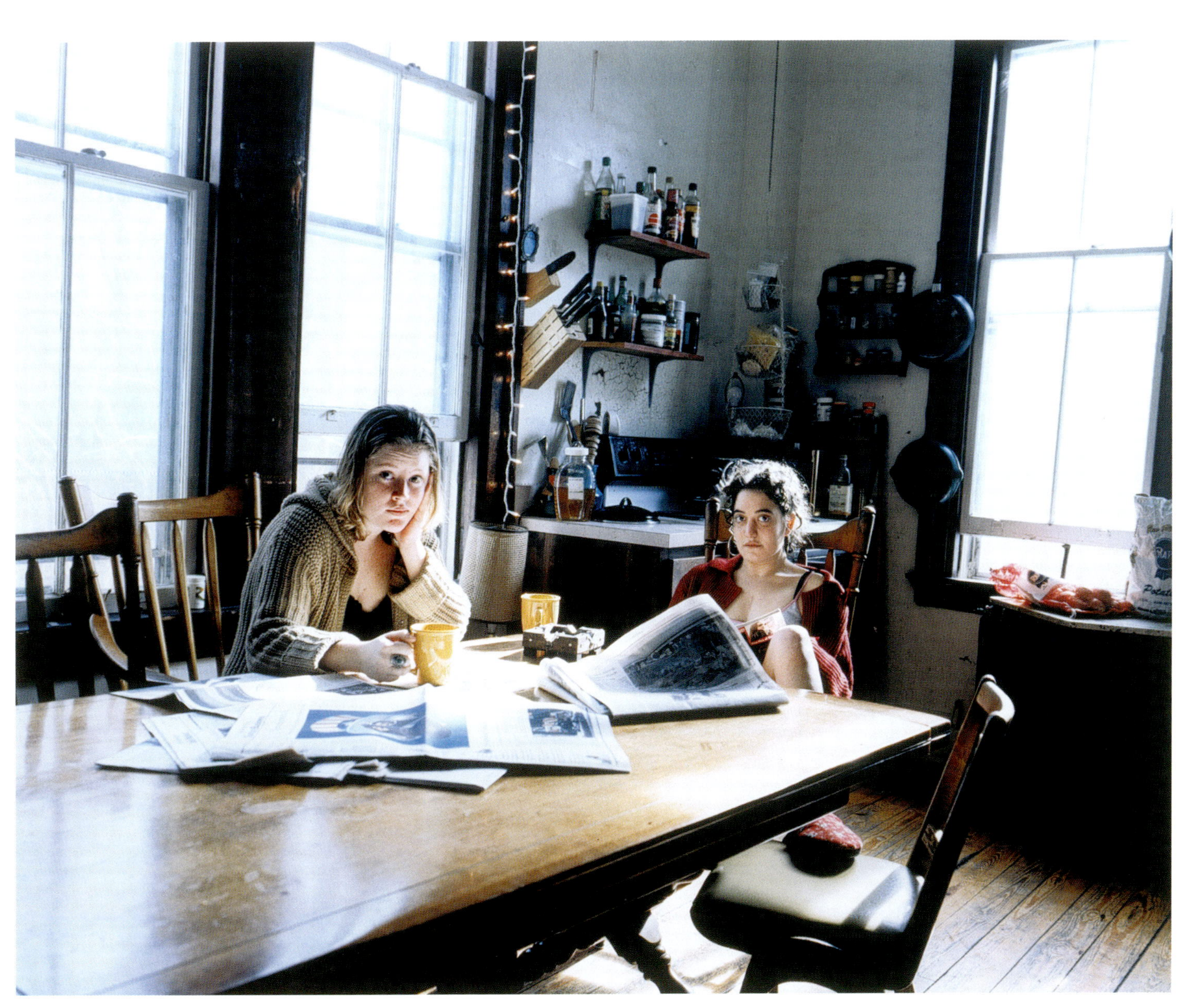

Exhibitors

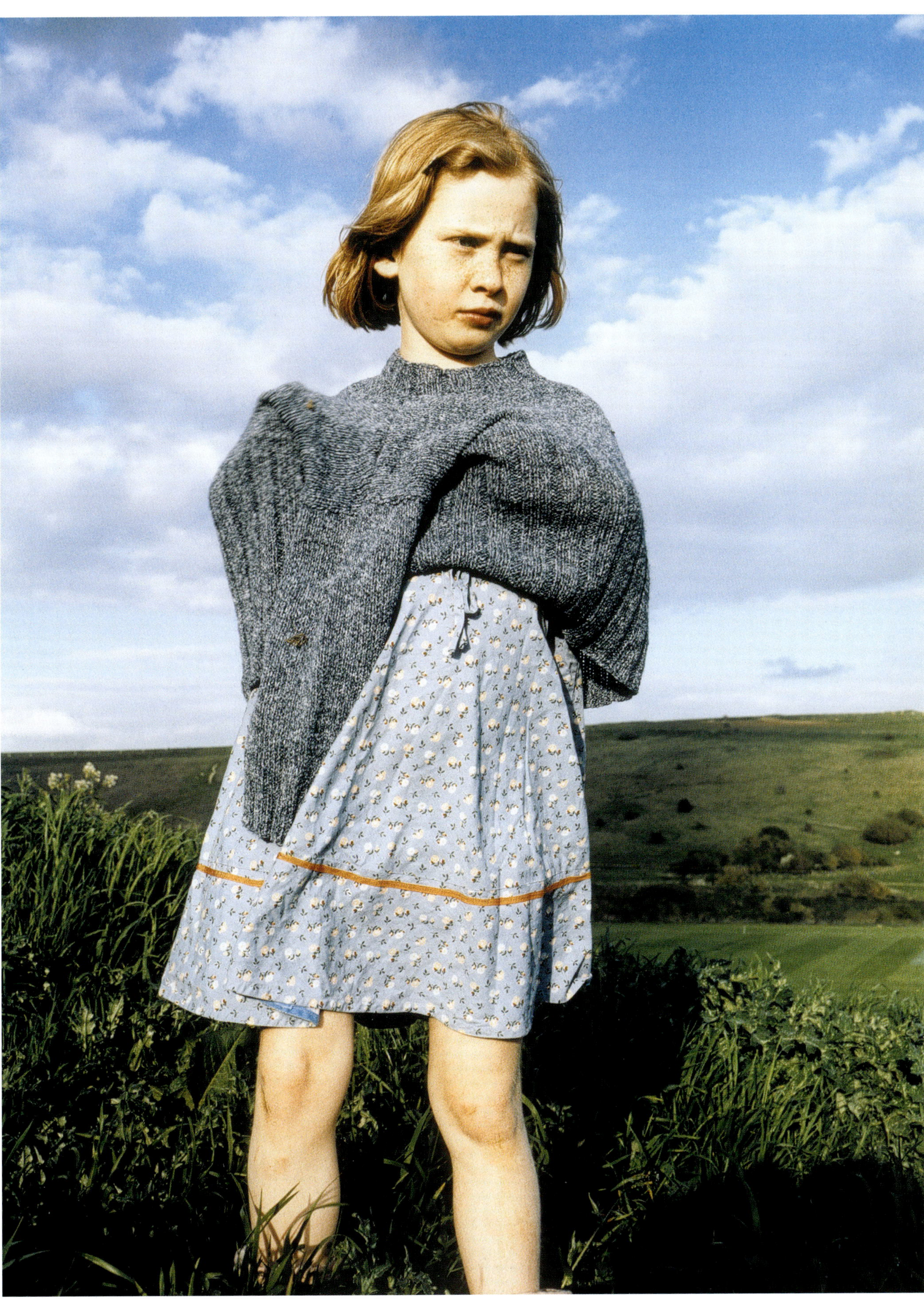

**Hiroshi
Watanabe**

Portrait #05
from the series
**Ideology
in Paradise,
Portraits from
Pyongyang
Schoolchildren's
Palace,
North Korea**
April 2006

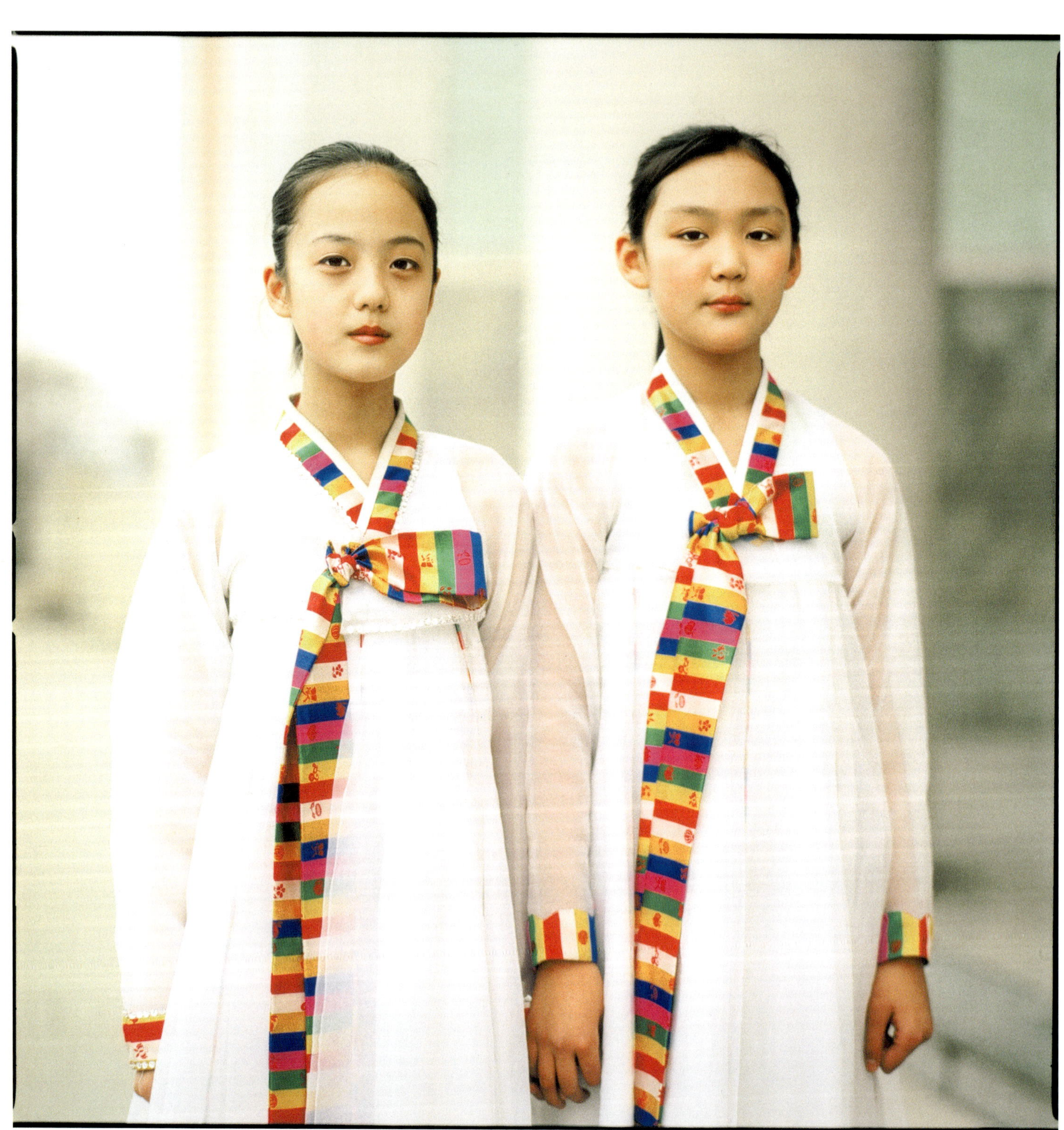

Ljudmilla Socci   Chiara
from the series
Portraits
June 2005

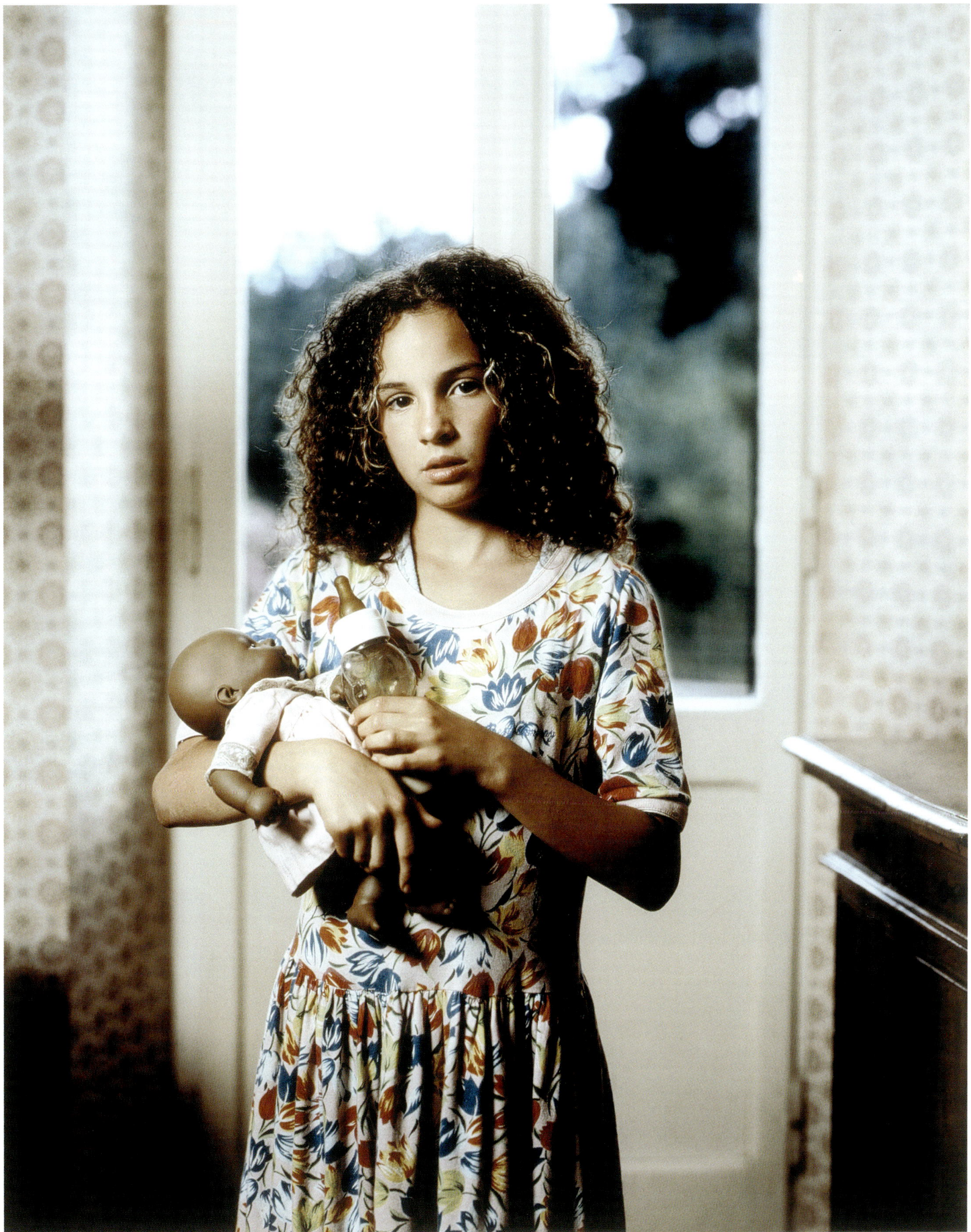

**Madeleine
Waller**

Sophie Hannah
from the series
**Portraits
of Poets**
November 2005

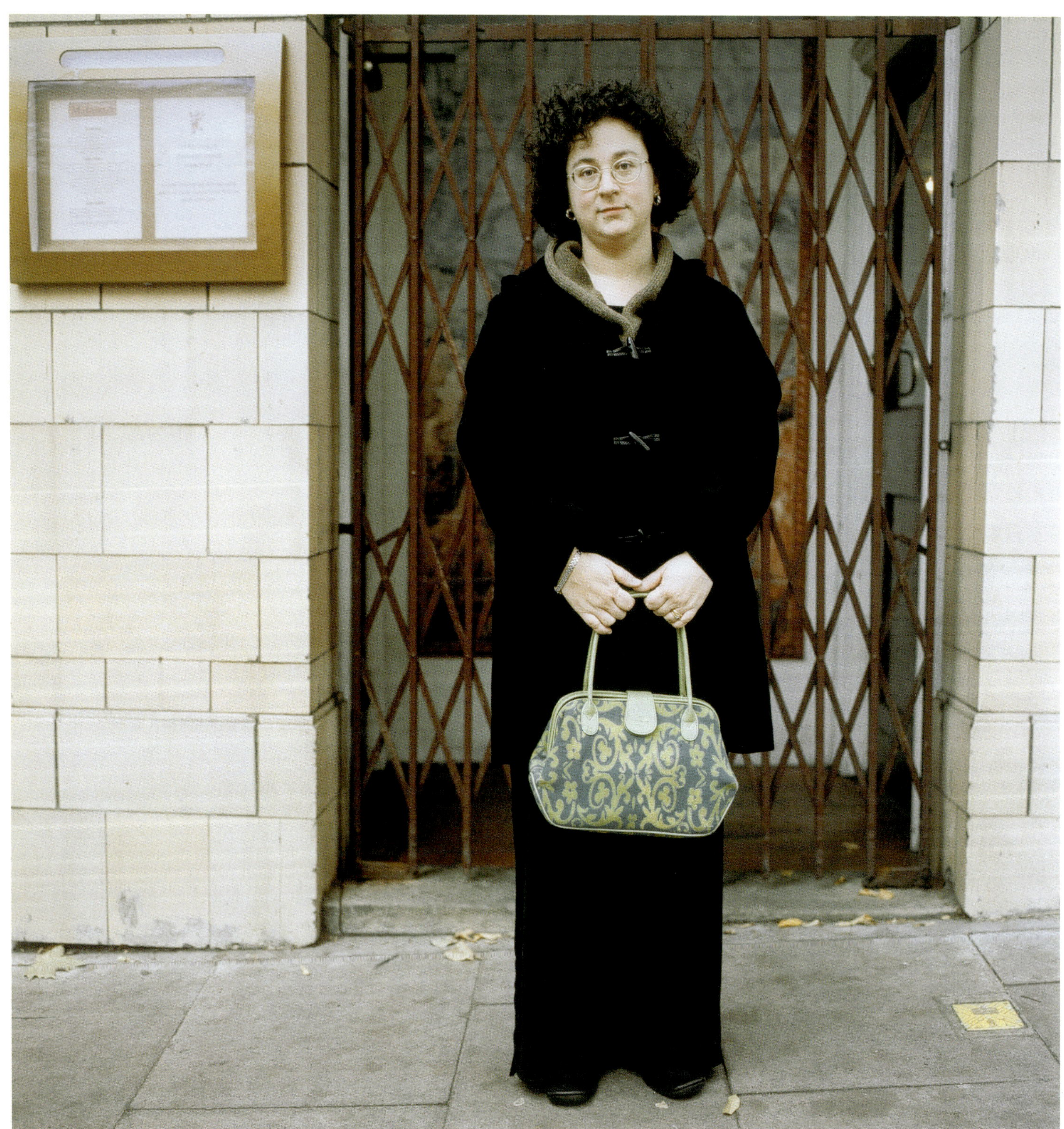

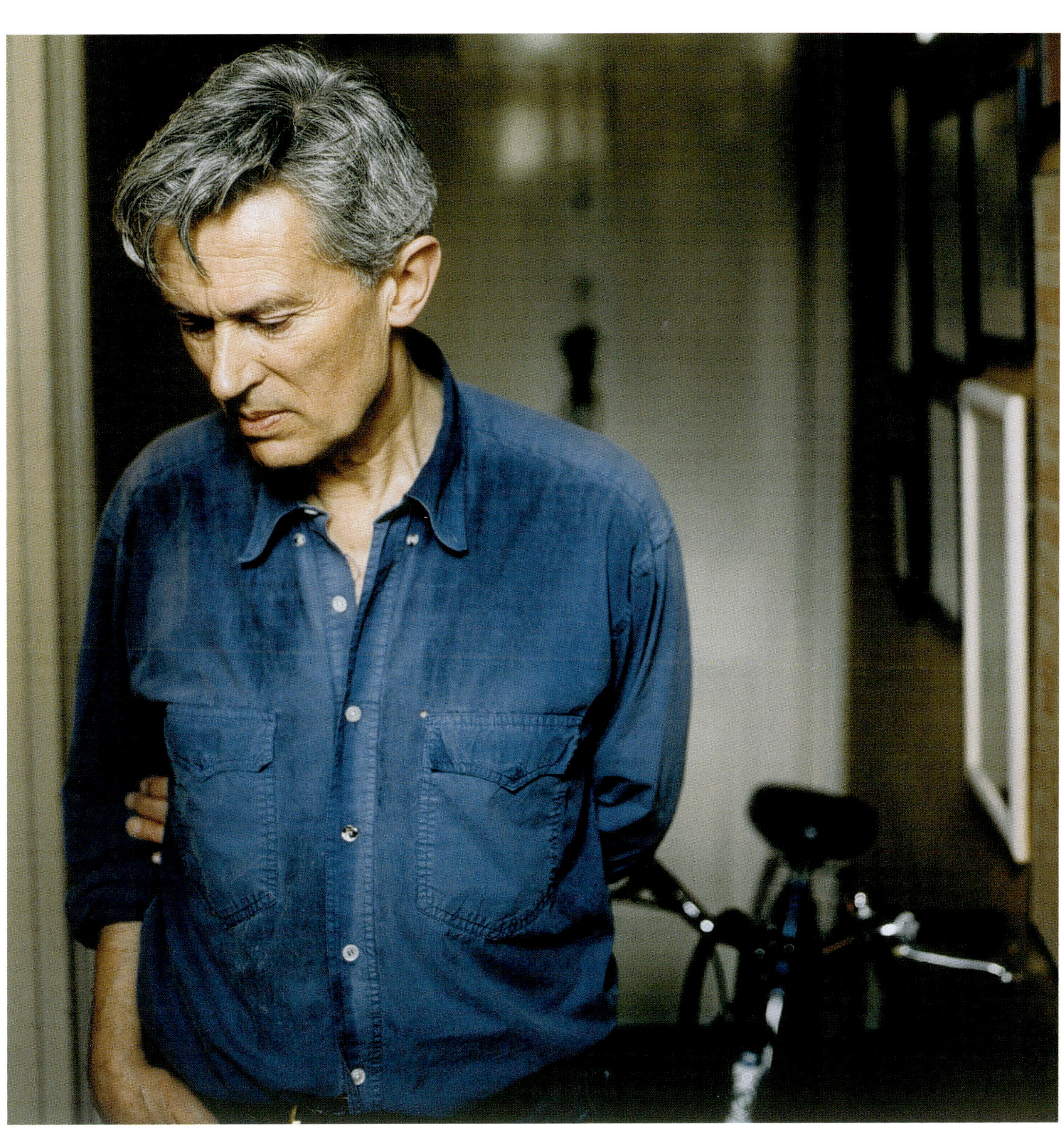

Bernd Edgar Wichmann   Sascha
August 2005

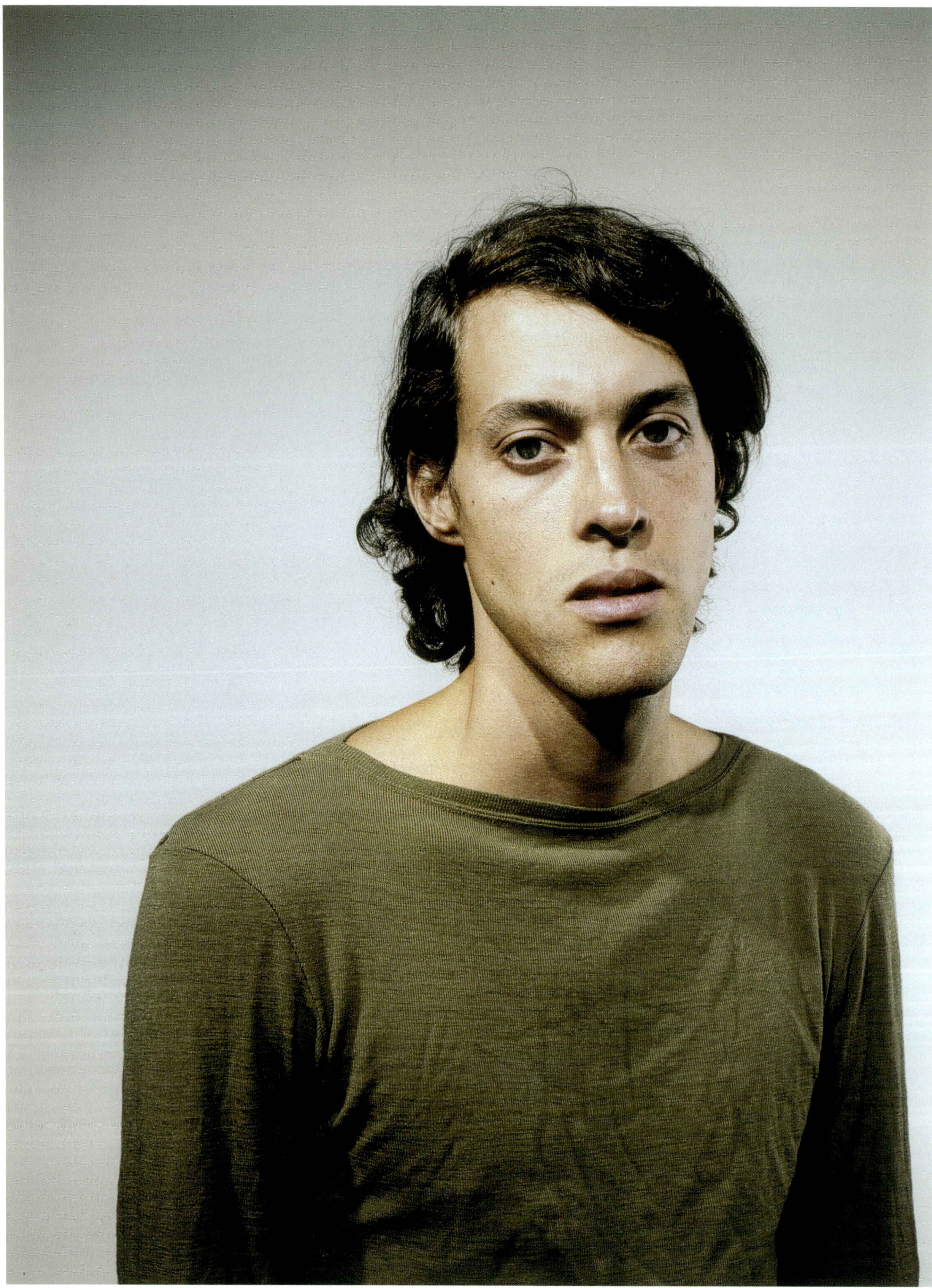

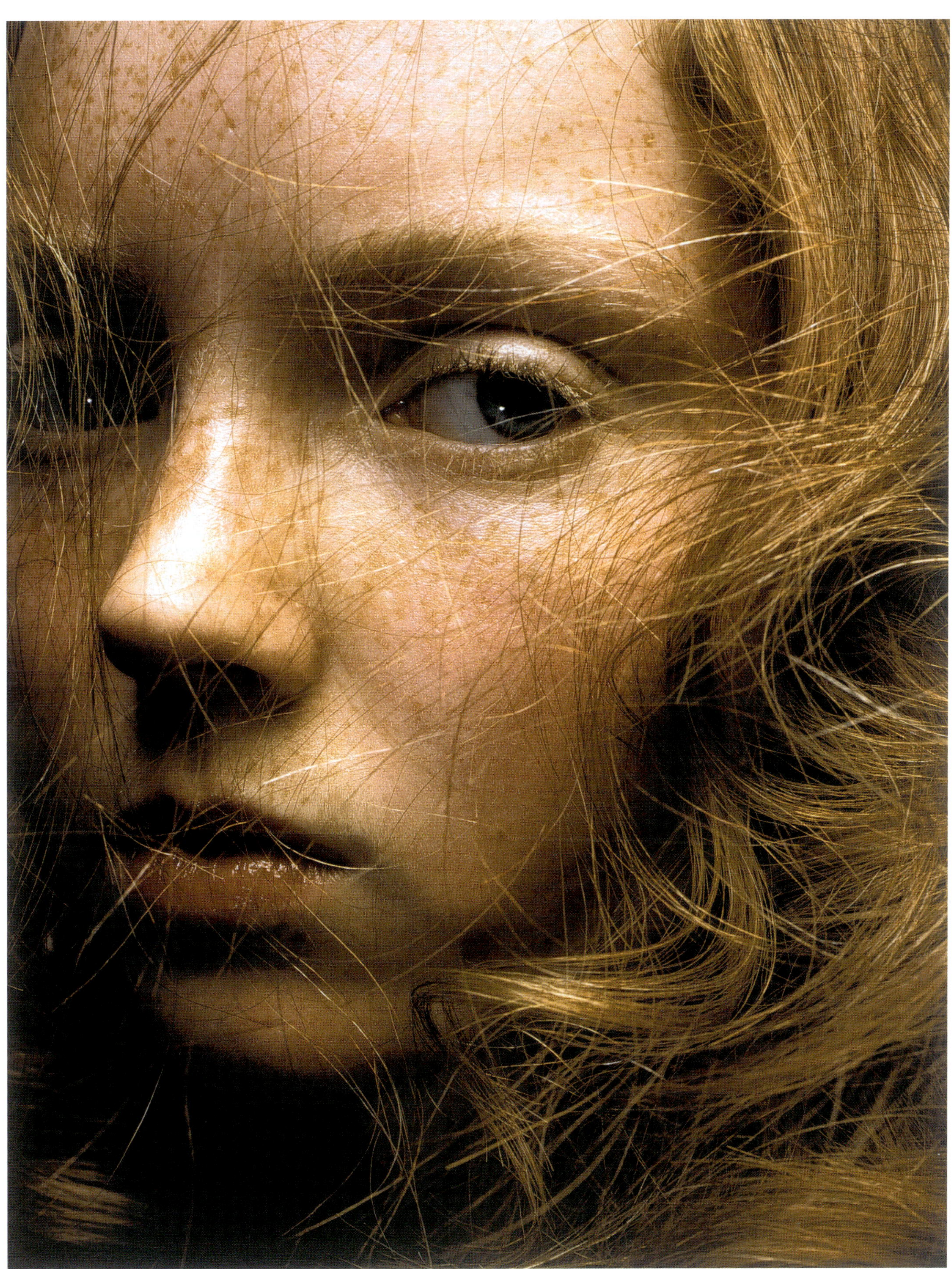

Eitan Lee Al   Lily as
Elizabeth I
February 2005

Lek
Kiatsirikajorn

Mom
June 2006

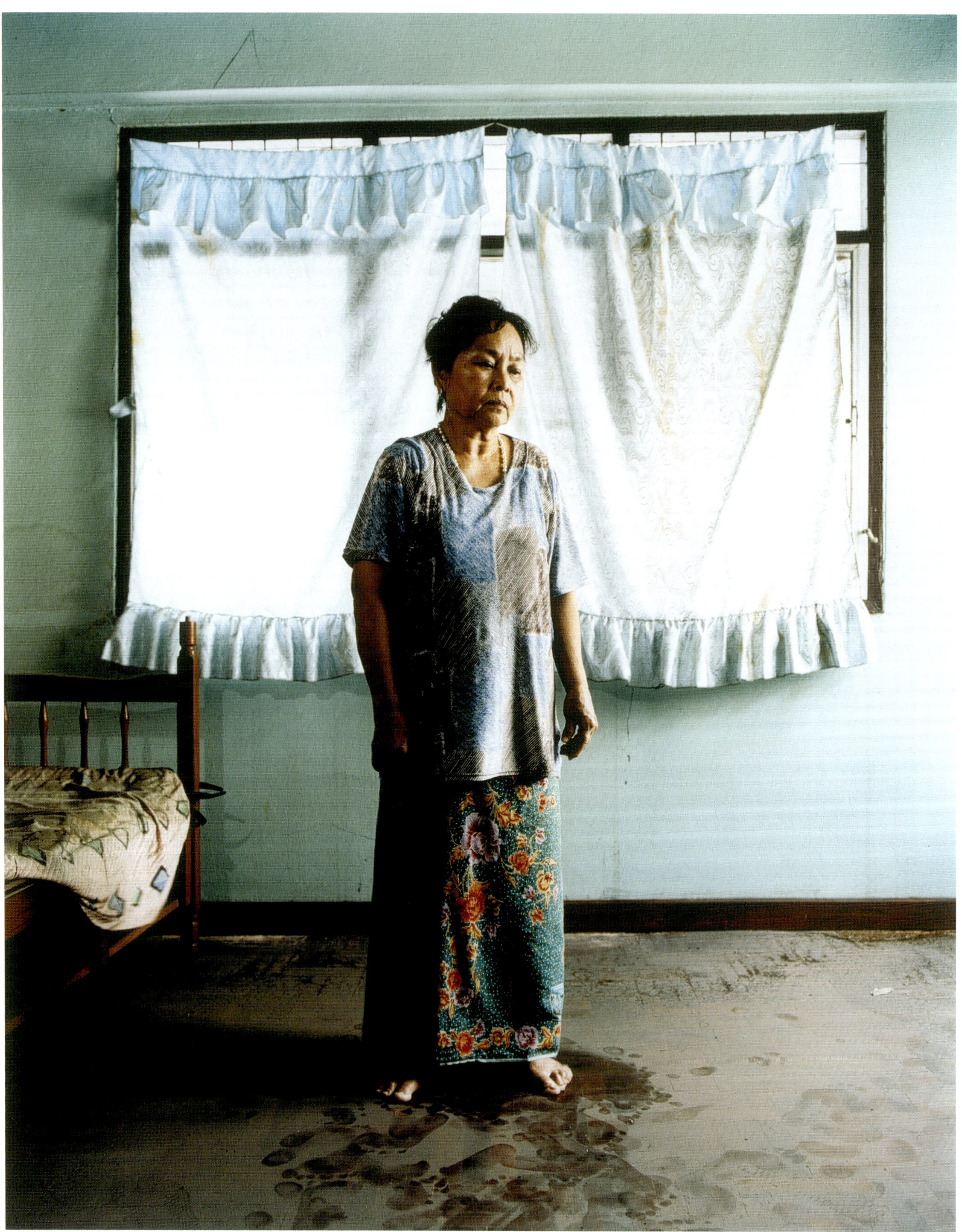

James
Pomerantz

Pakistan Boy #1
from the series
After the Quake
December 2005

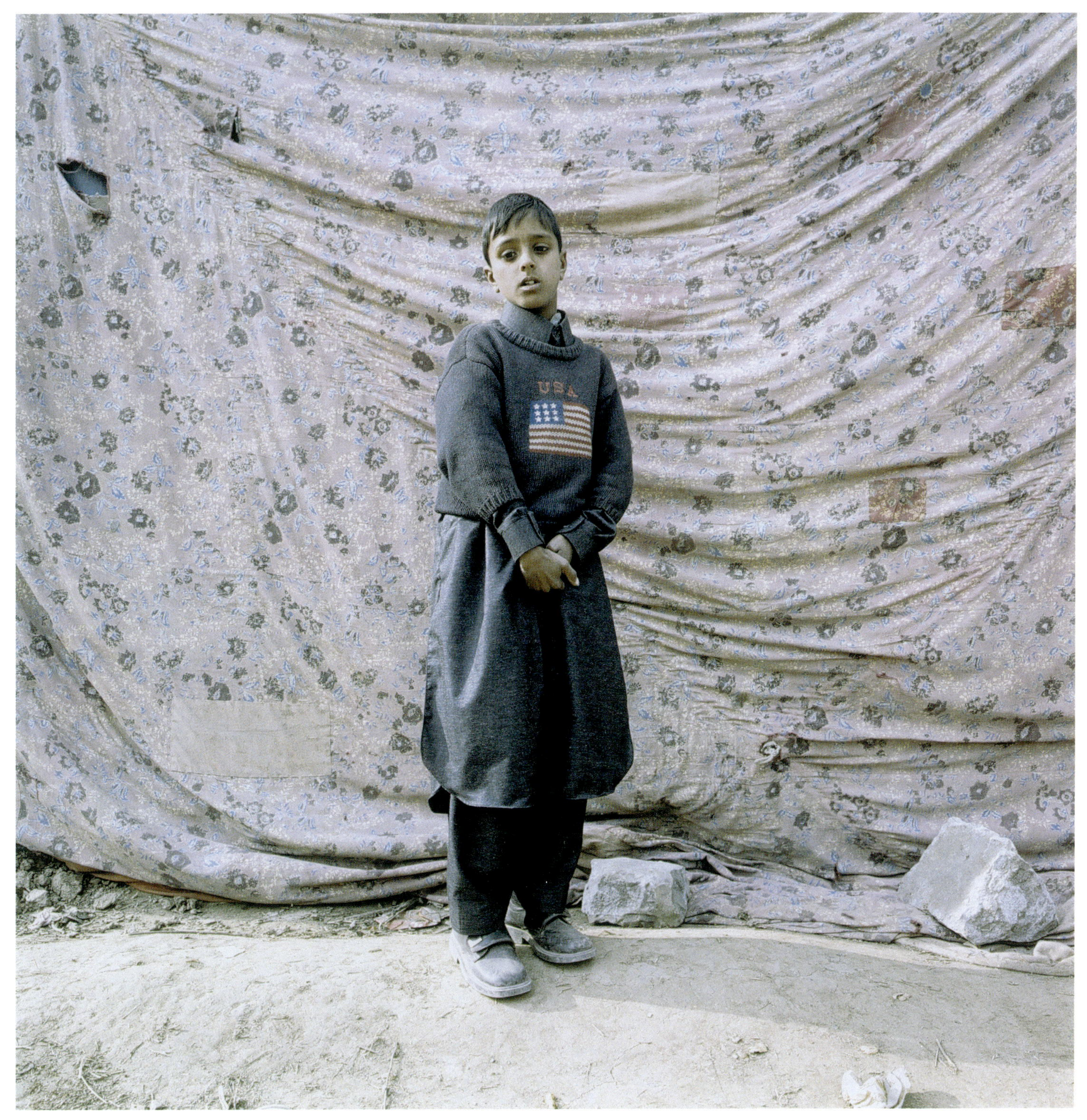

Andrew
Buurman

Untitled
from the series
Uplands
Allotments
September
2005

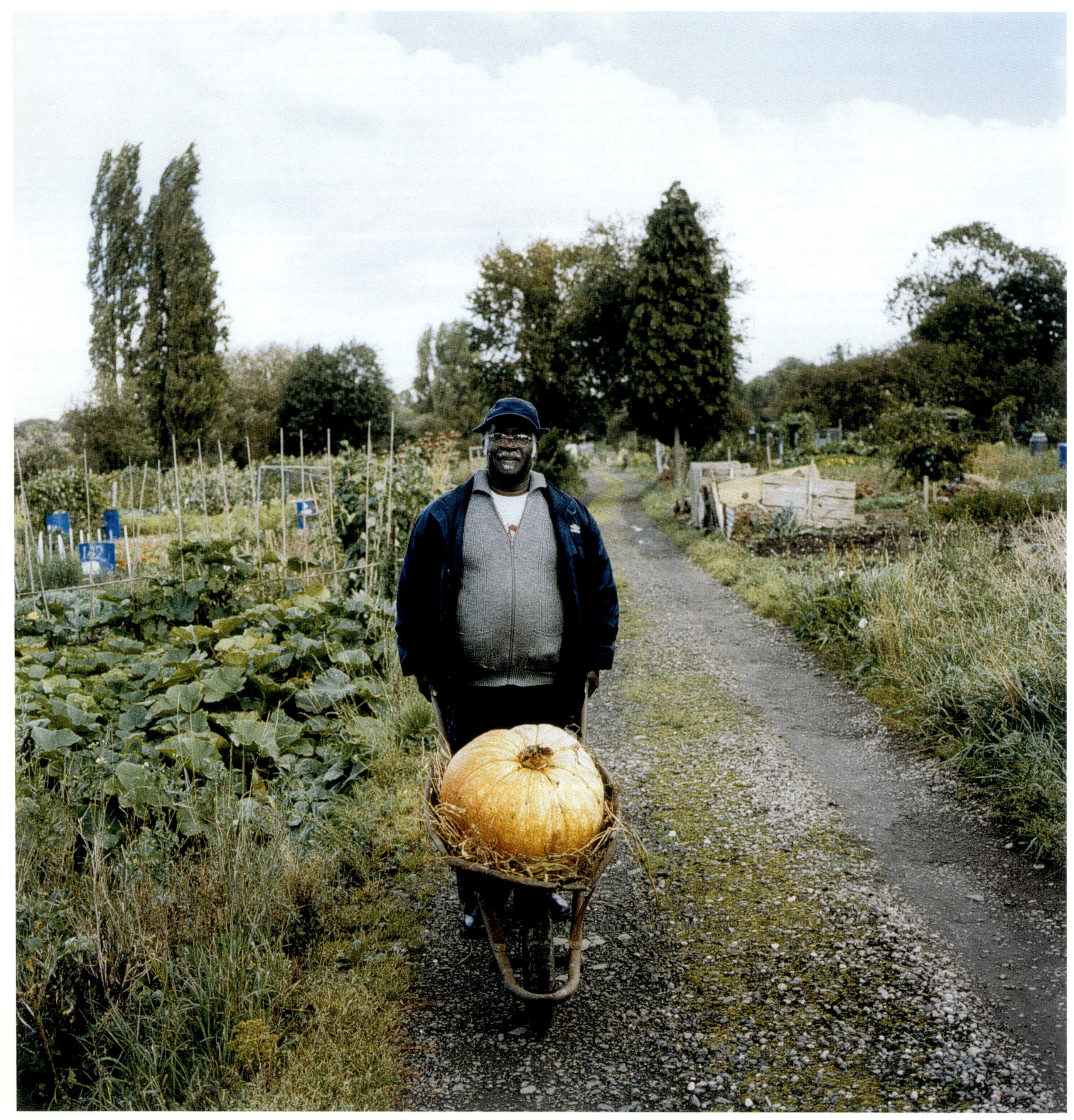

Monika Merva Mariann,
Hungary
from the series
City of Children,
Hungary
May 2005

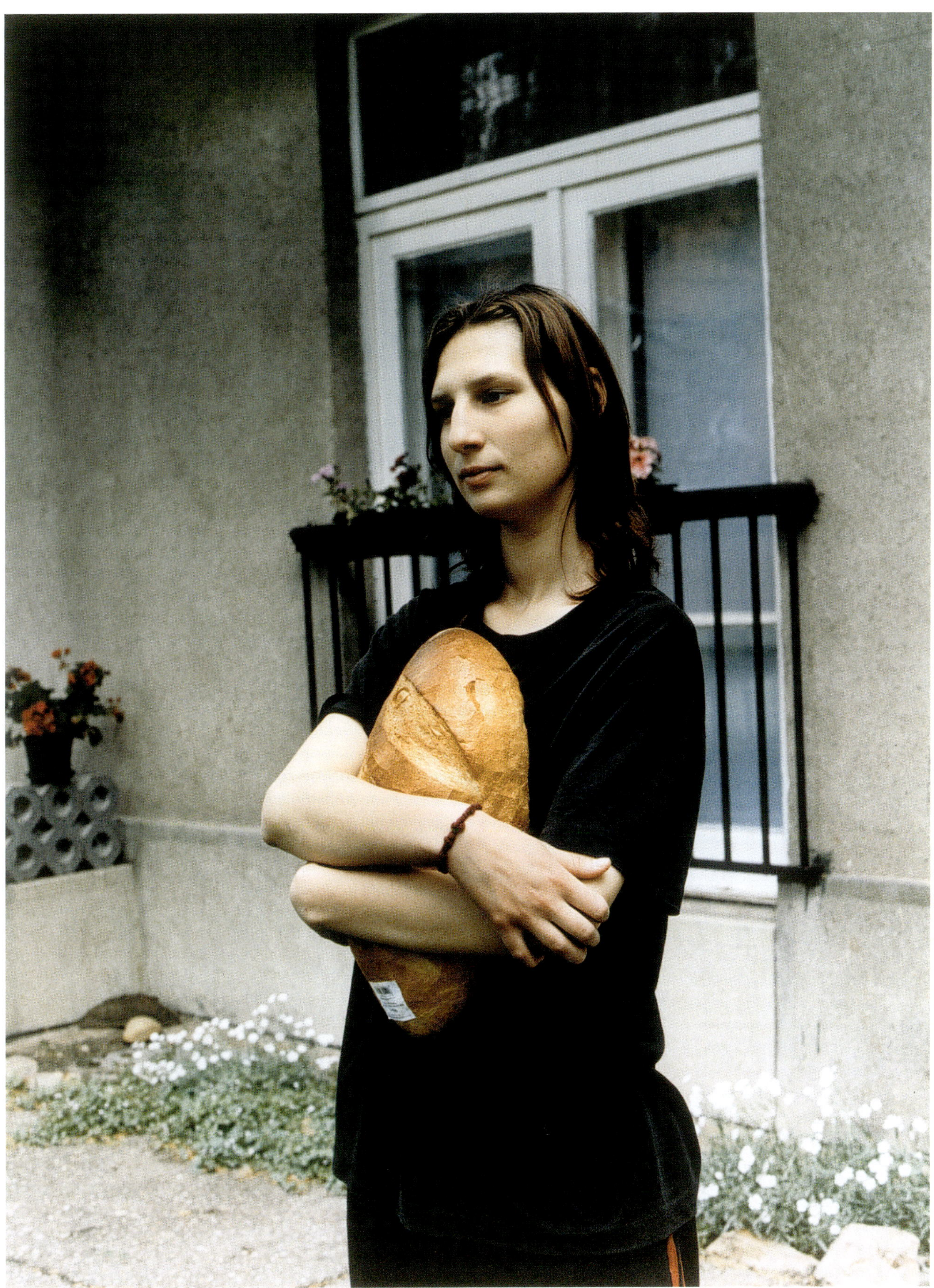

Kiryl Smaliakou The Morning
After, Belarus
July 2005

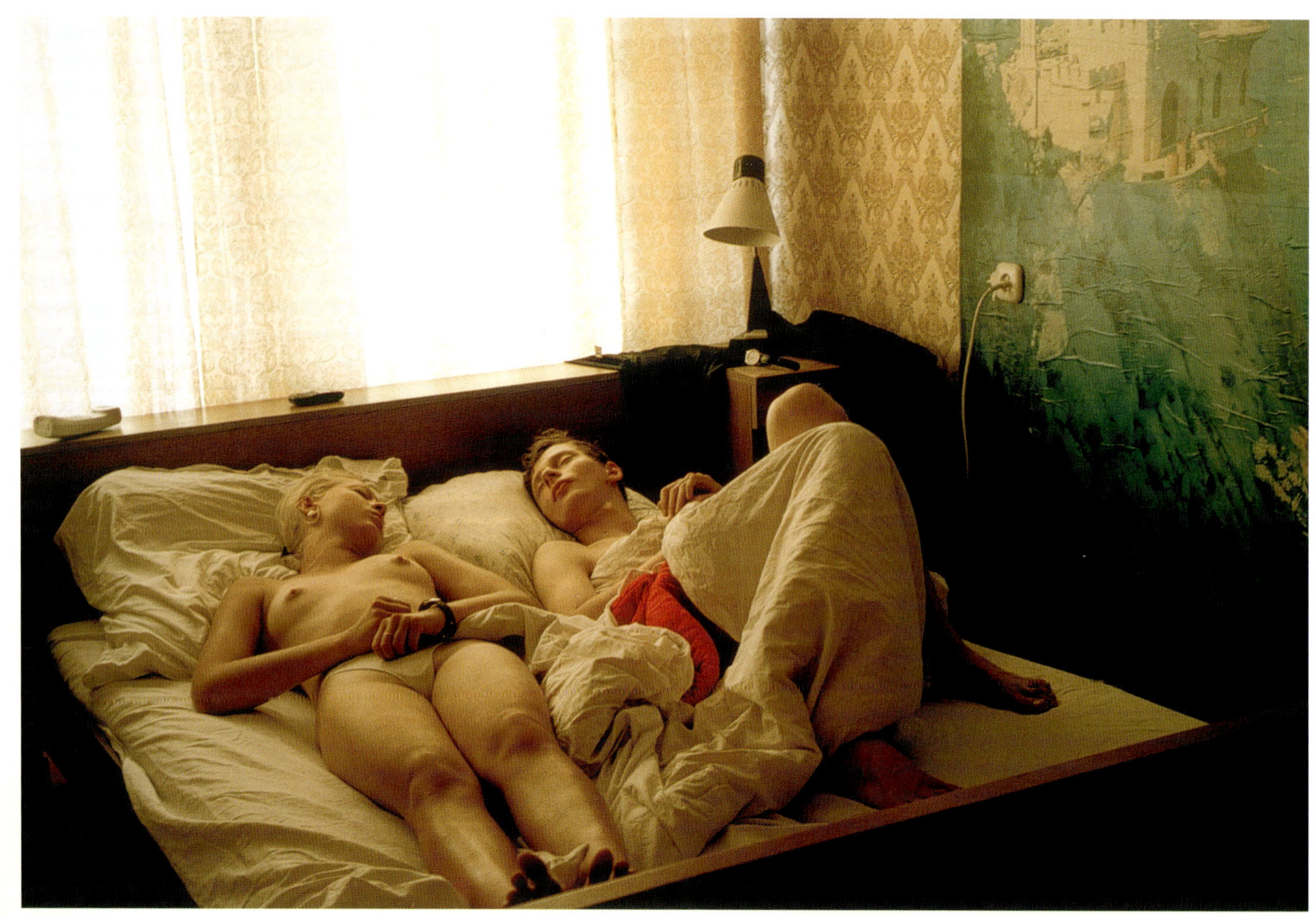

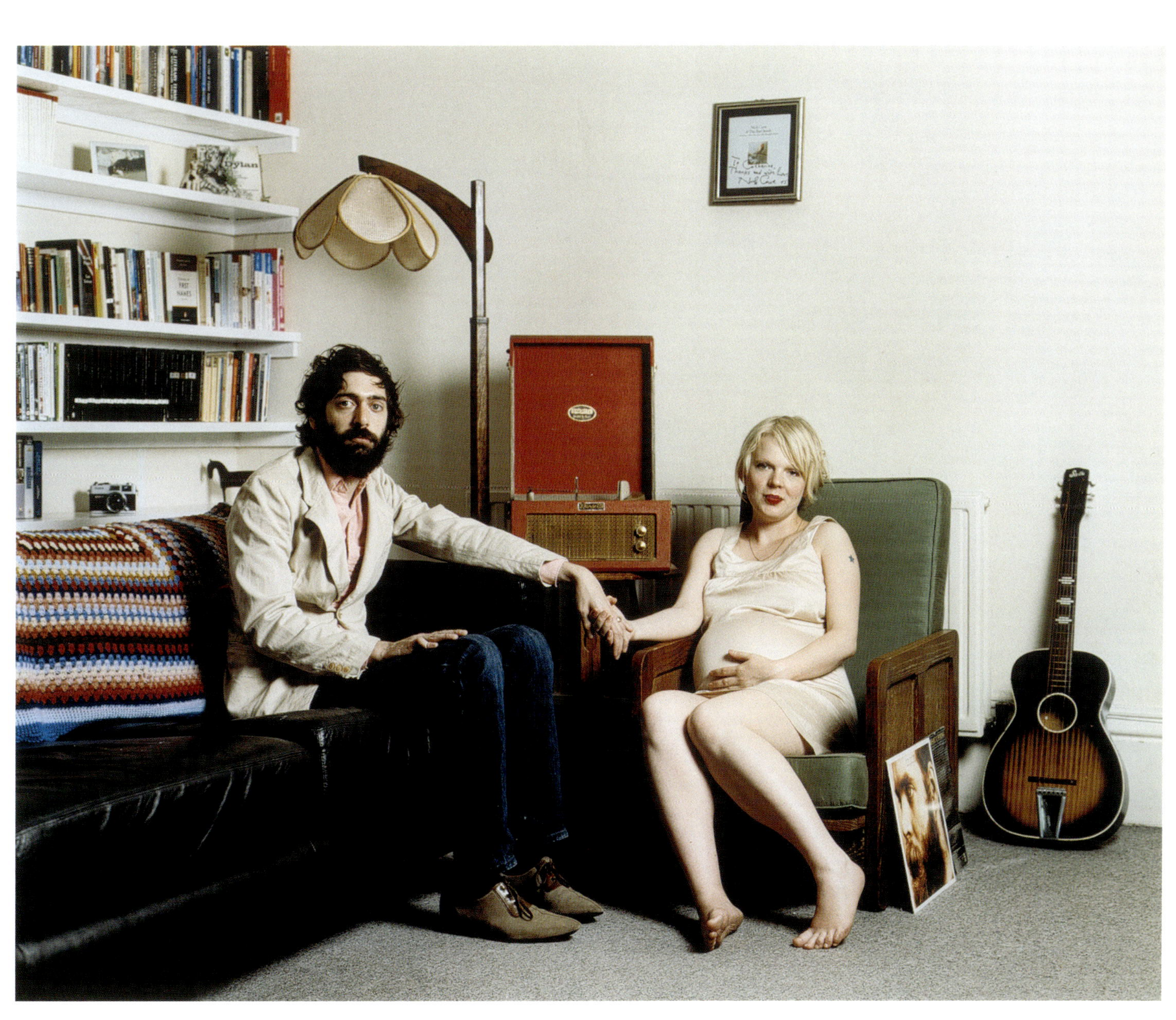

Michal Chelbin Sasha, an Orphan Boy in Practice, Ukraine 2005 *from the series* Strangely Familiar September 2005

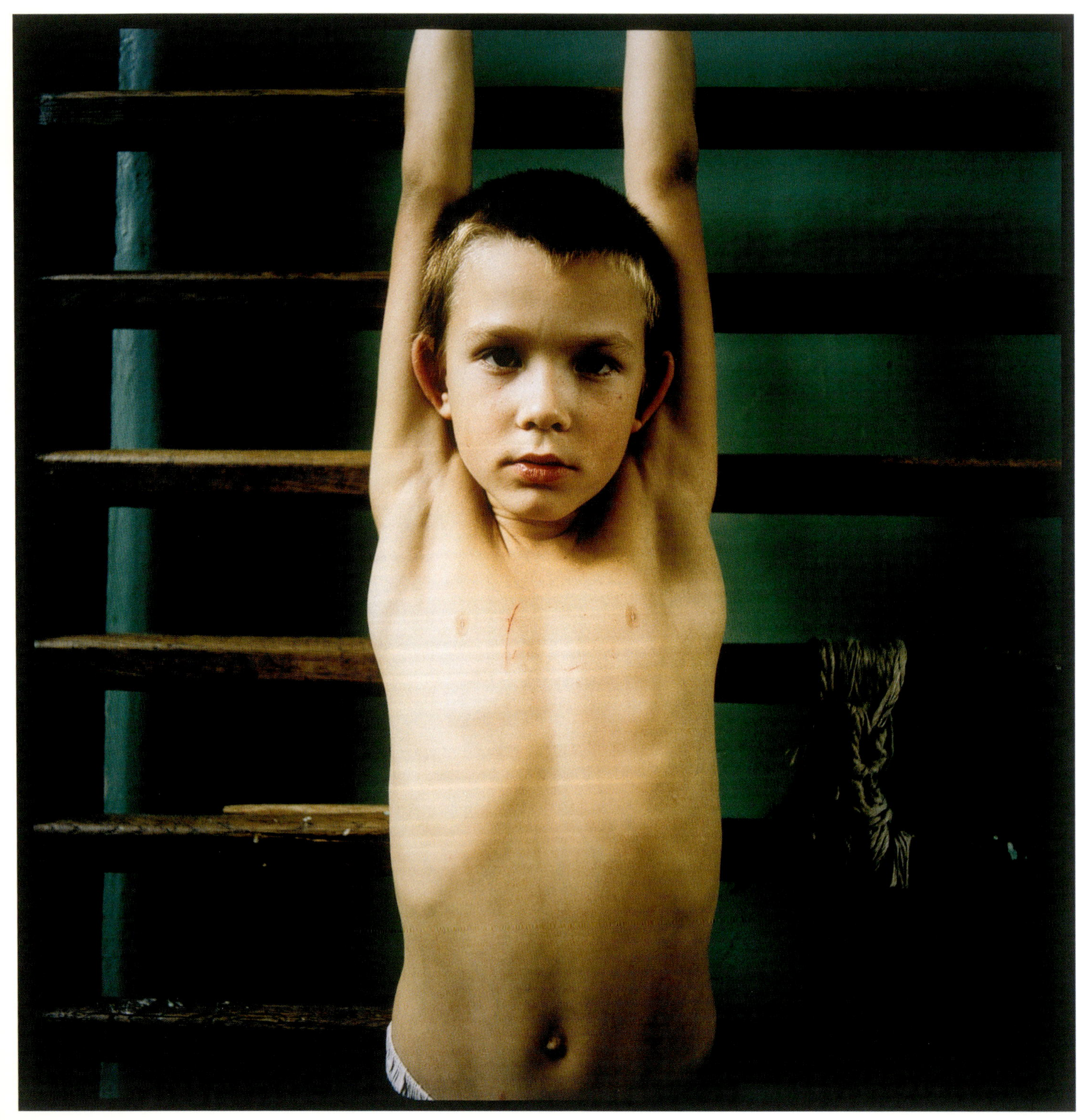

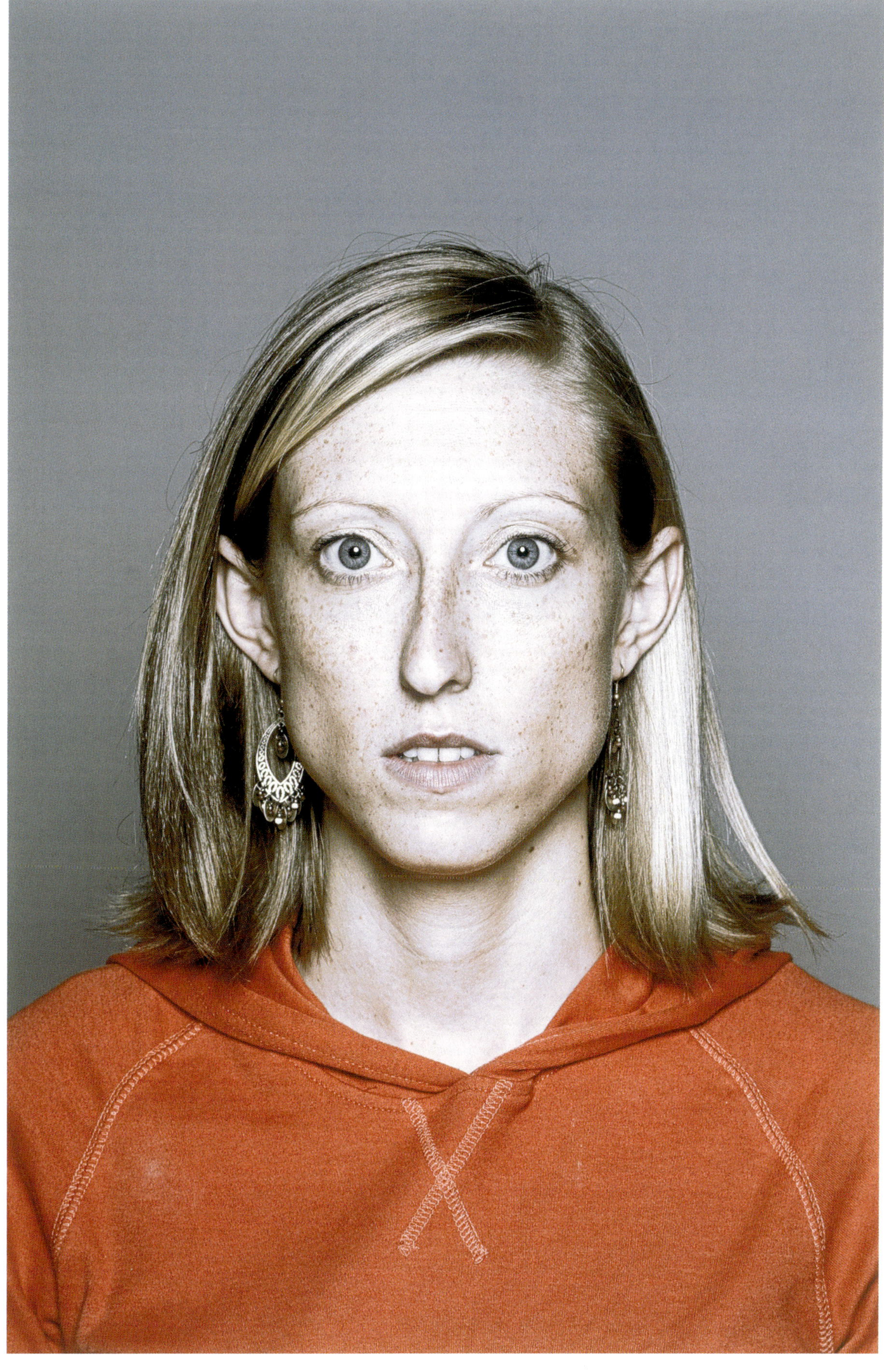

Christopher
Lane

Amused
from the series
Forbidden
February 2006

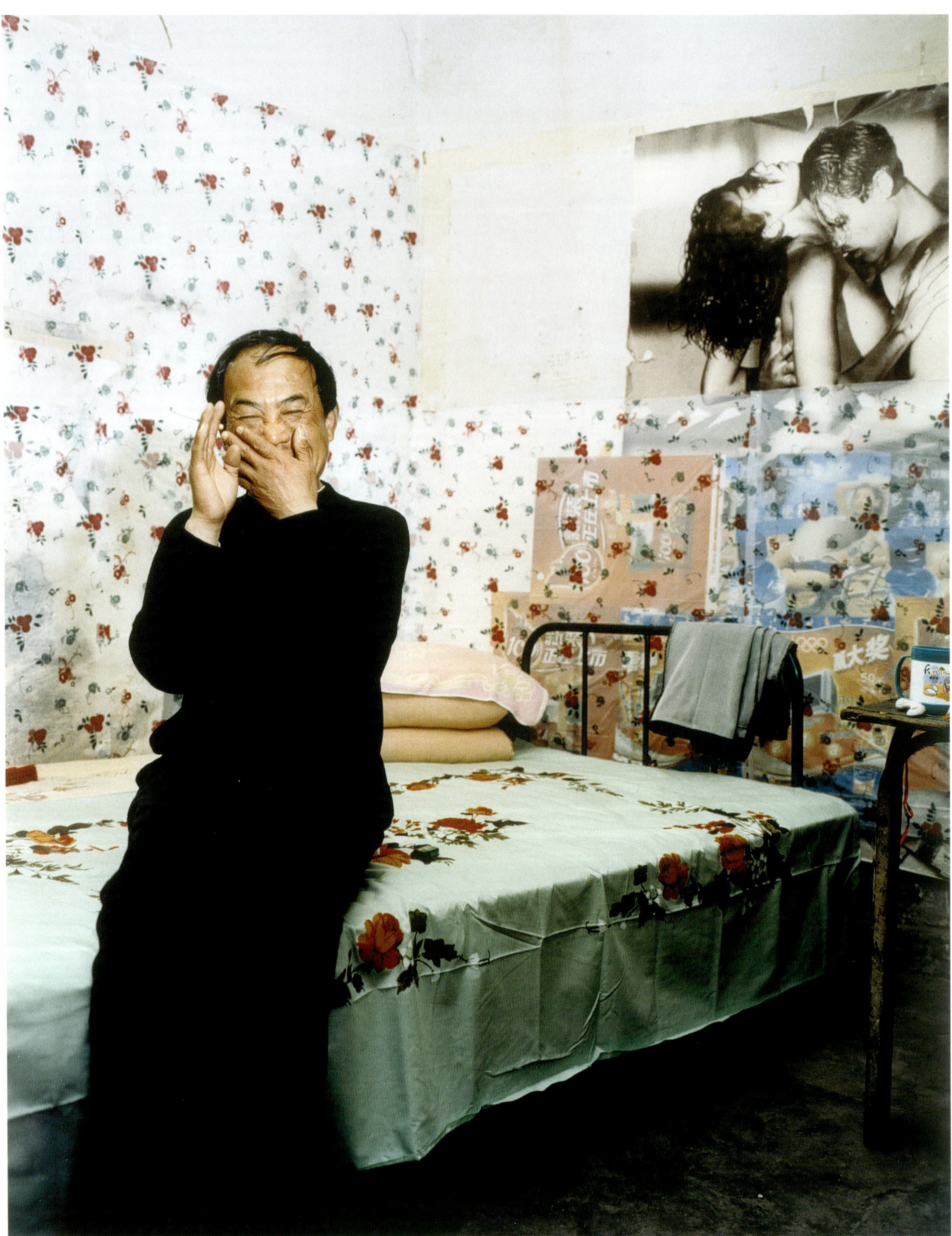

Clare Brannen   **Anne and Oli**
July 2006

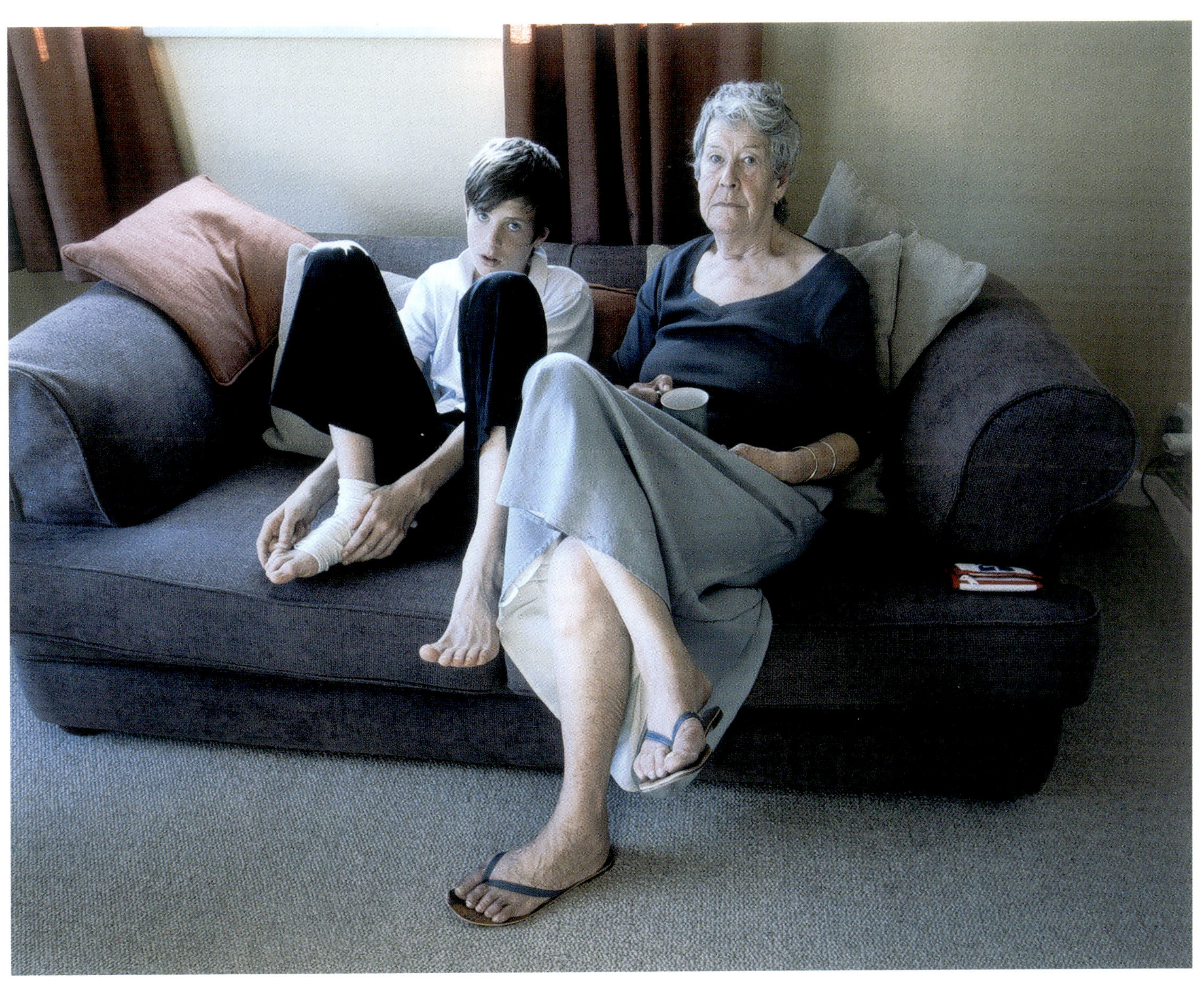

Moe Suzuki **Self-portrait**
from the series
**Christian
Identity Project**
February 2006

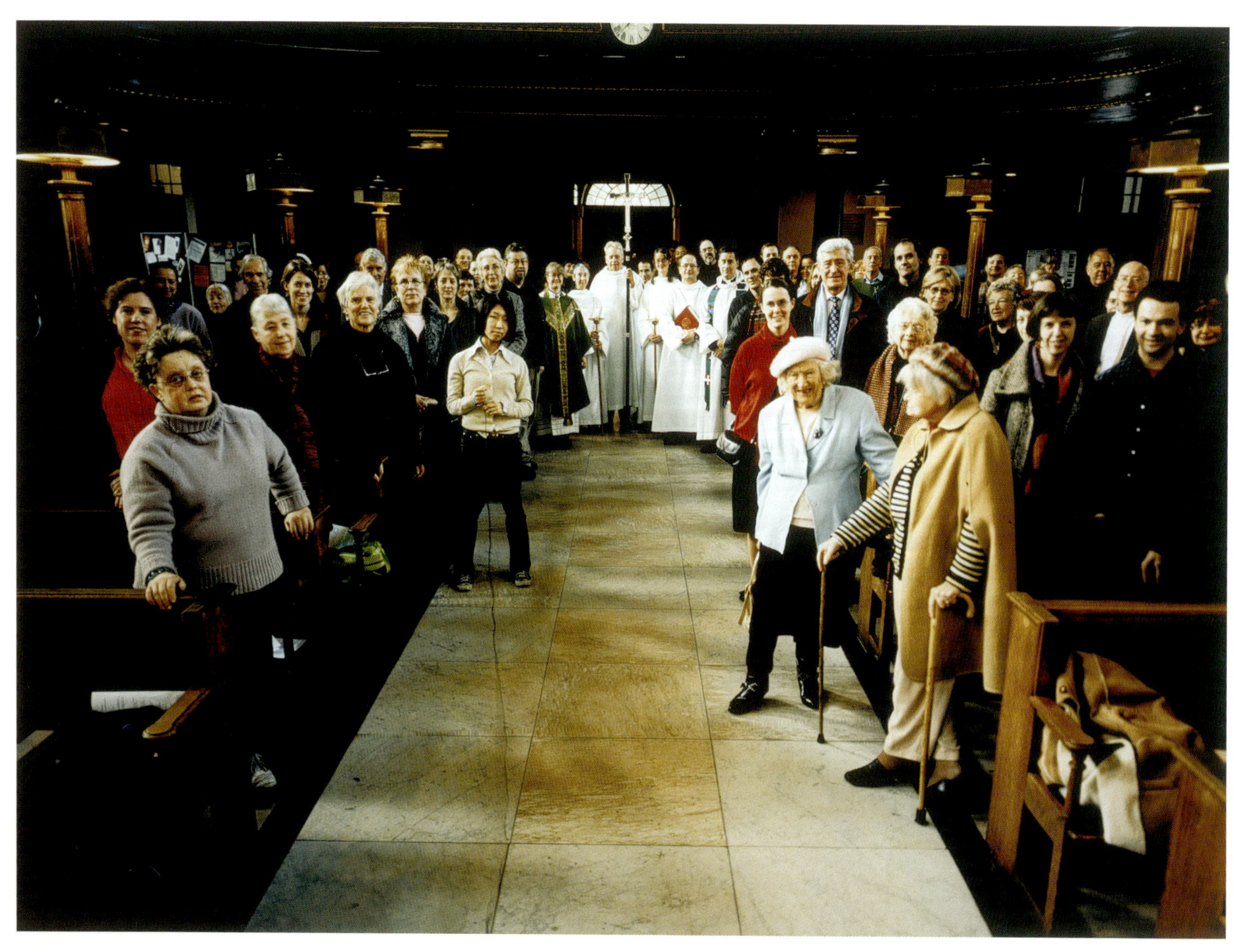

Jin Woo Kwon Group Portrait
of Cosplayers
January 2006

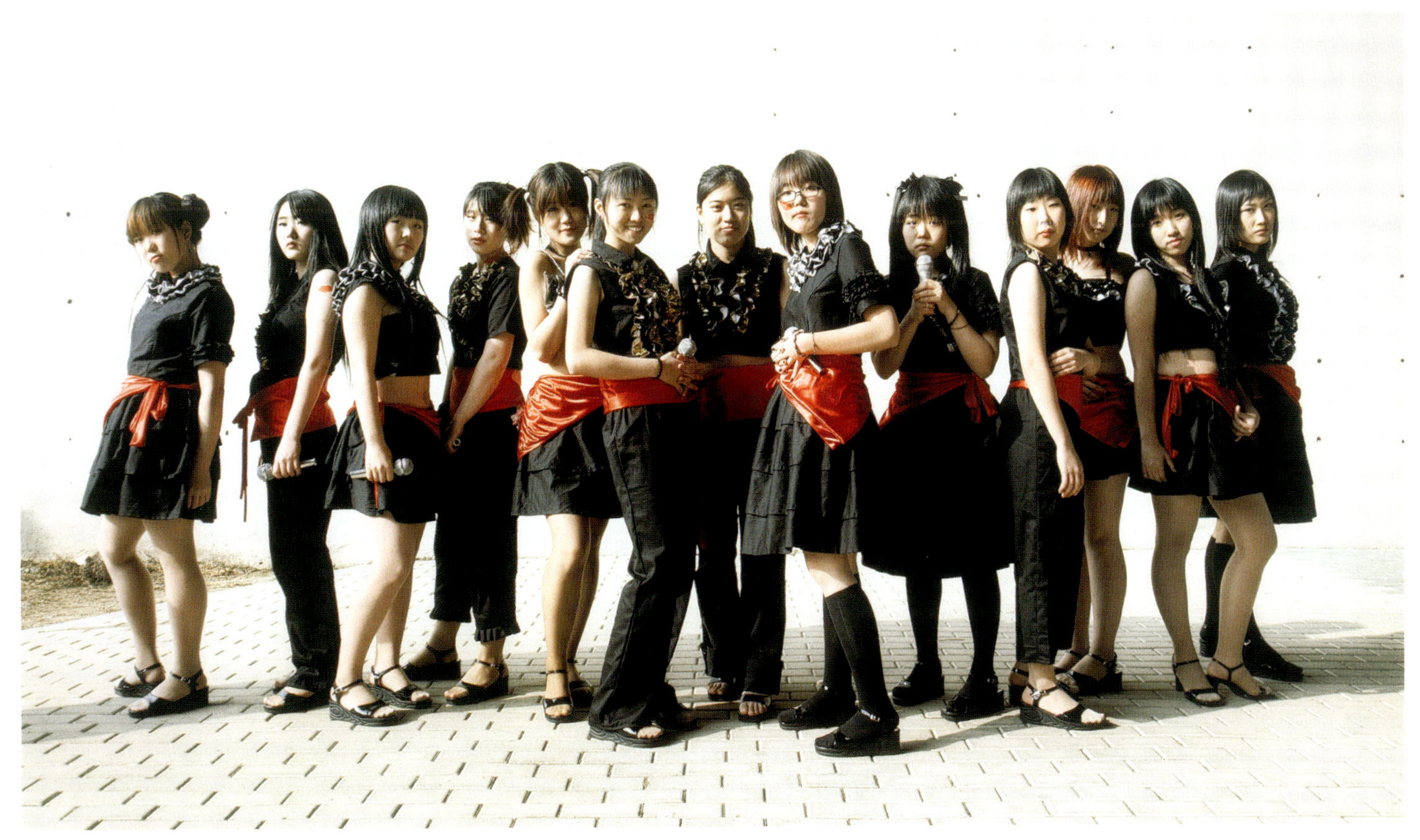

Steve Bloom   Hamar Woman,
Ethiopia
July 2005

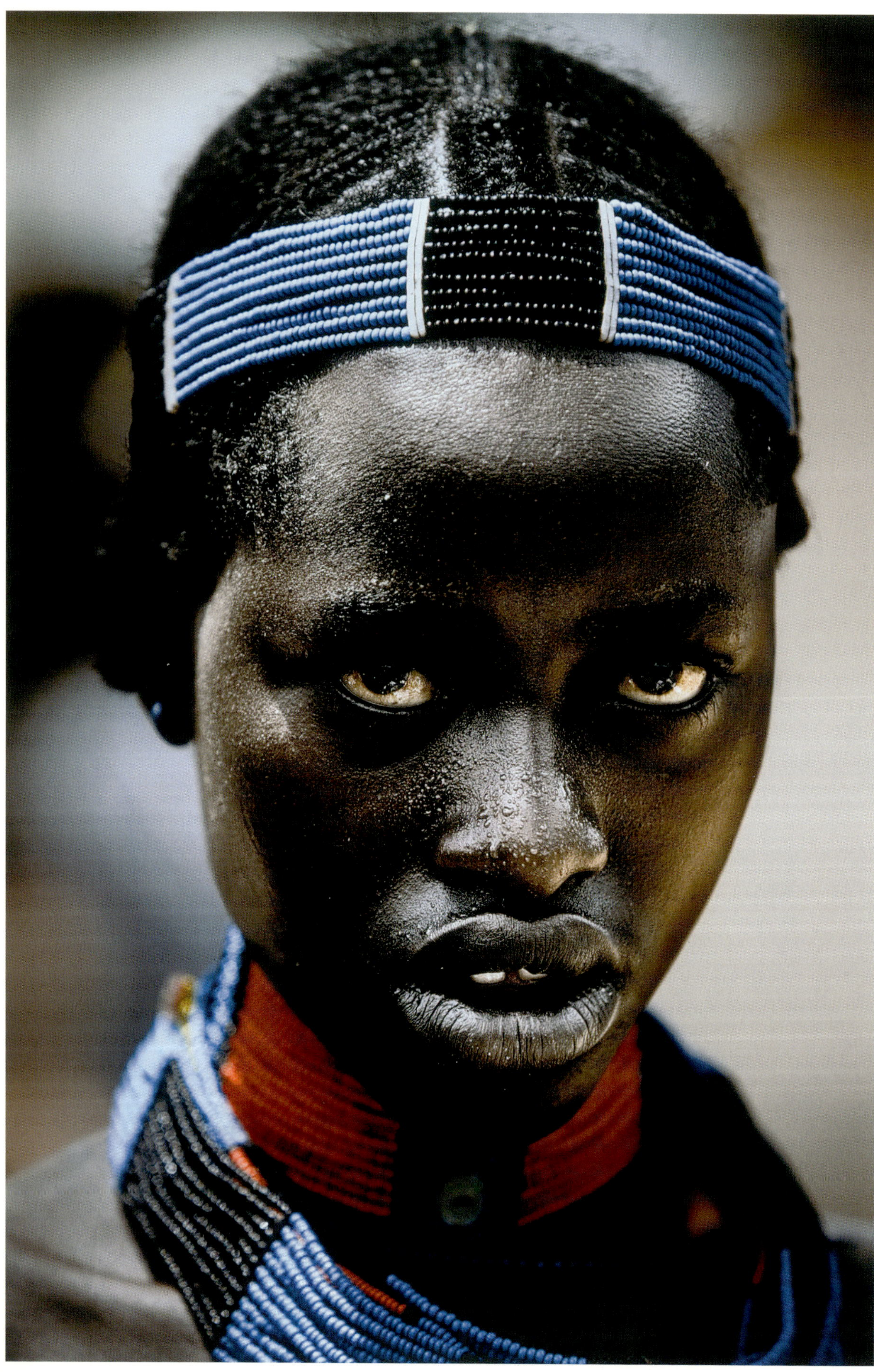

Steve Bloom Mursi Tribeswoman with Rifle, Ethiopia July 2005

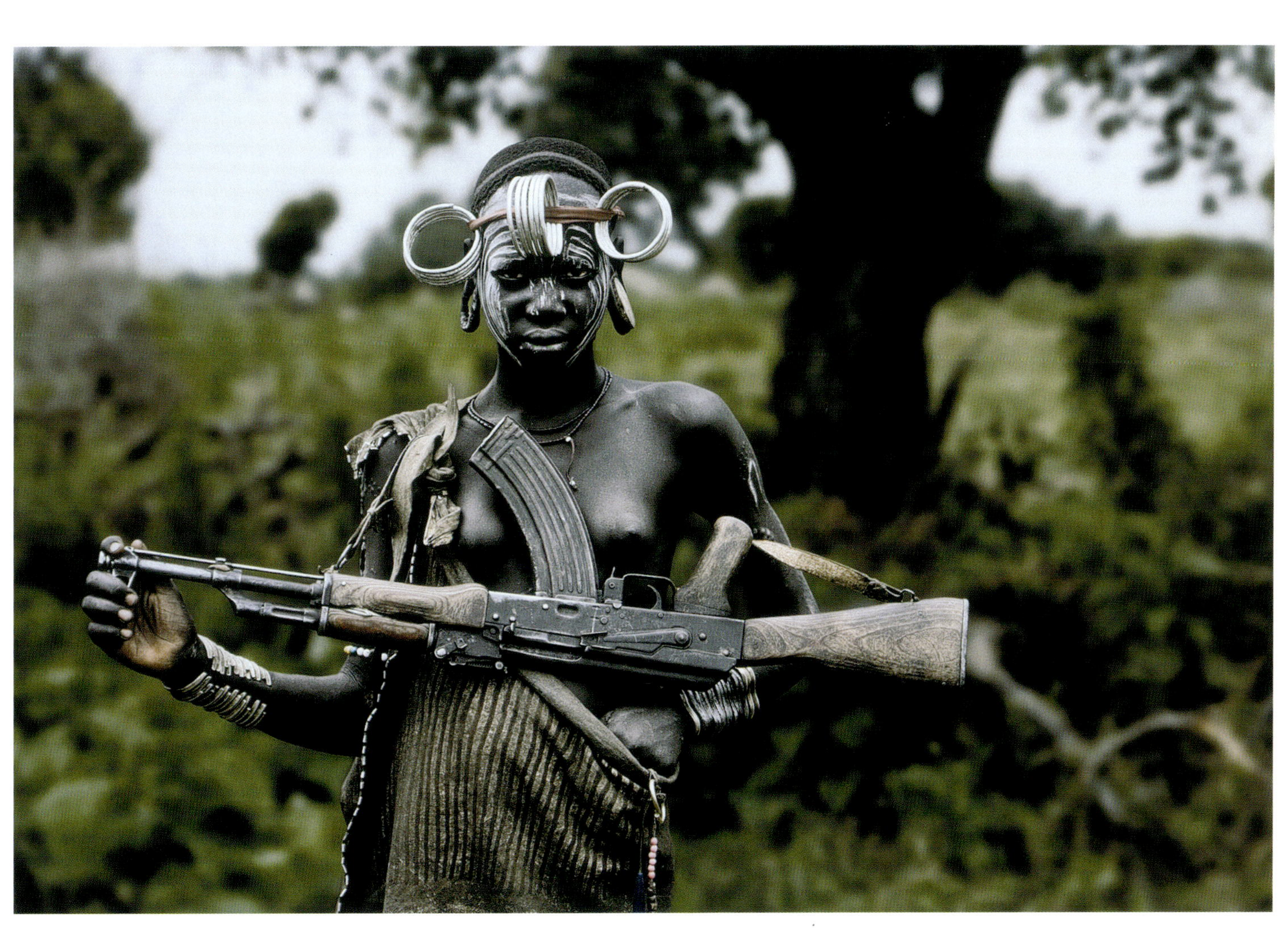

Desiree Pfeiffer Ian
September 2005

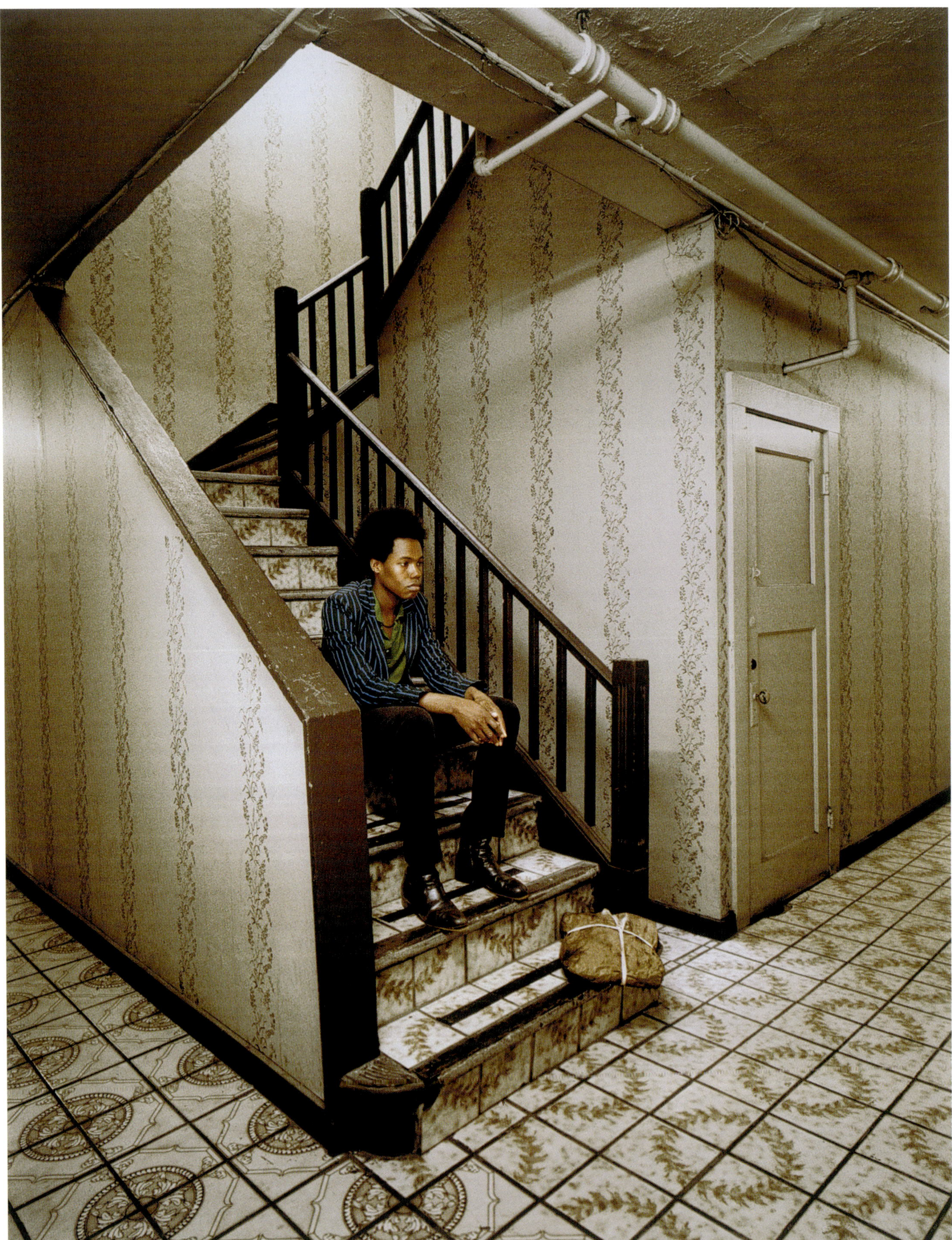

Mark Tedeschi Beijing Bun Boy
from the series
Beijing 2005
December 2005

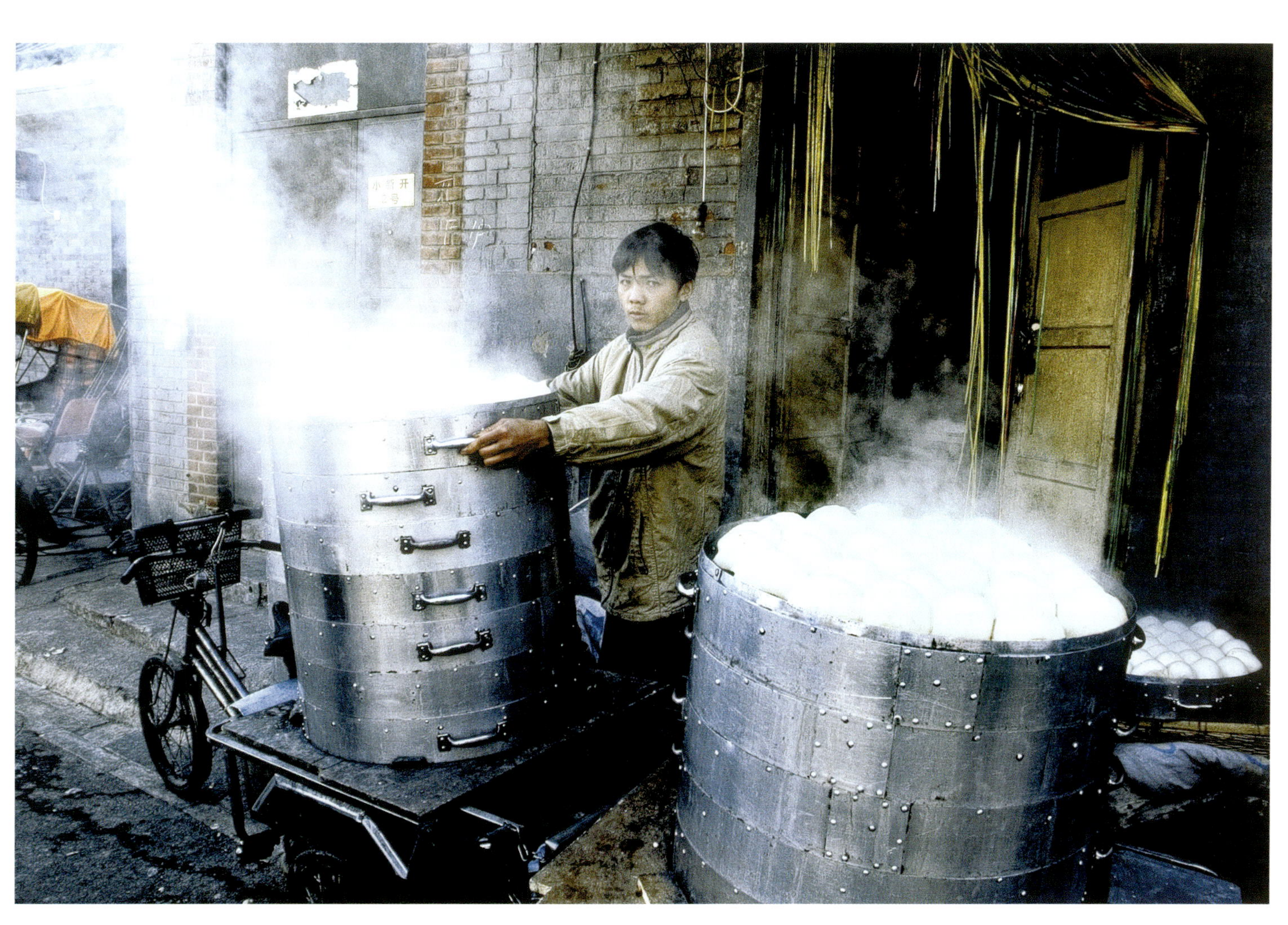

Charlie Crane   **Minye**
June 2006

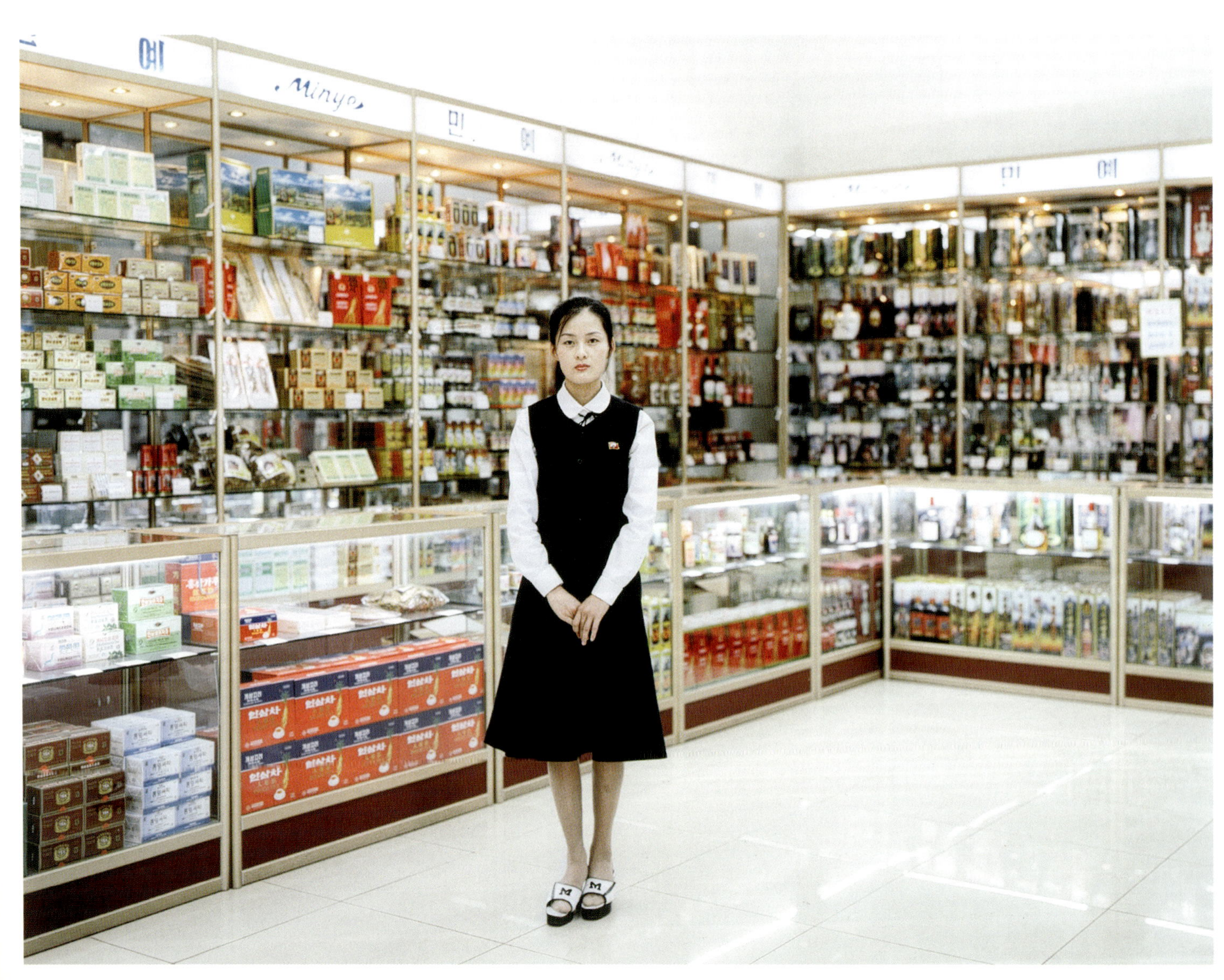

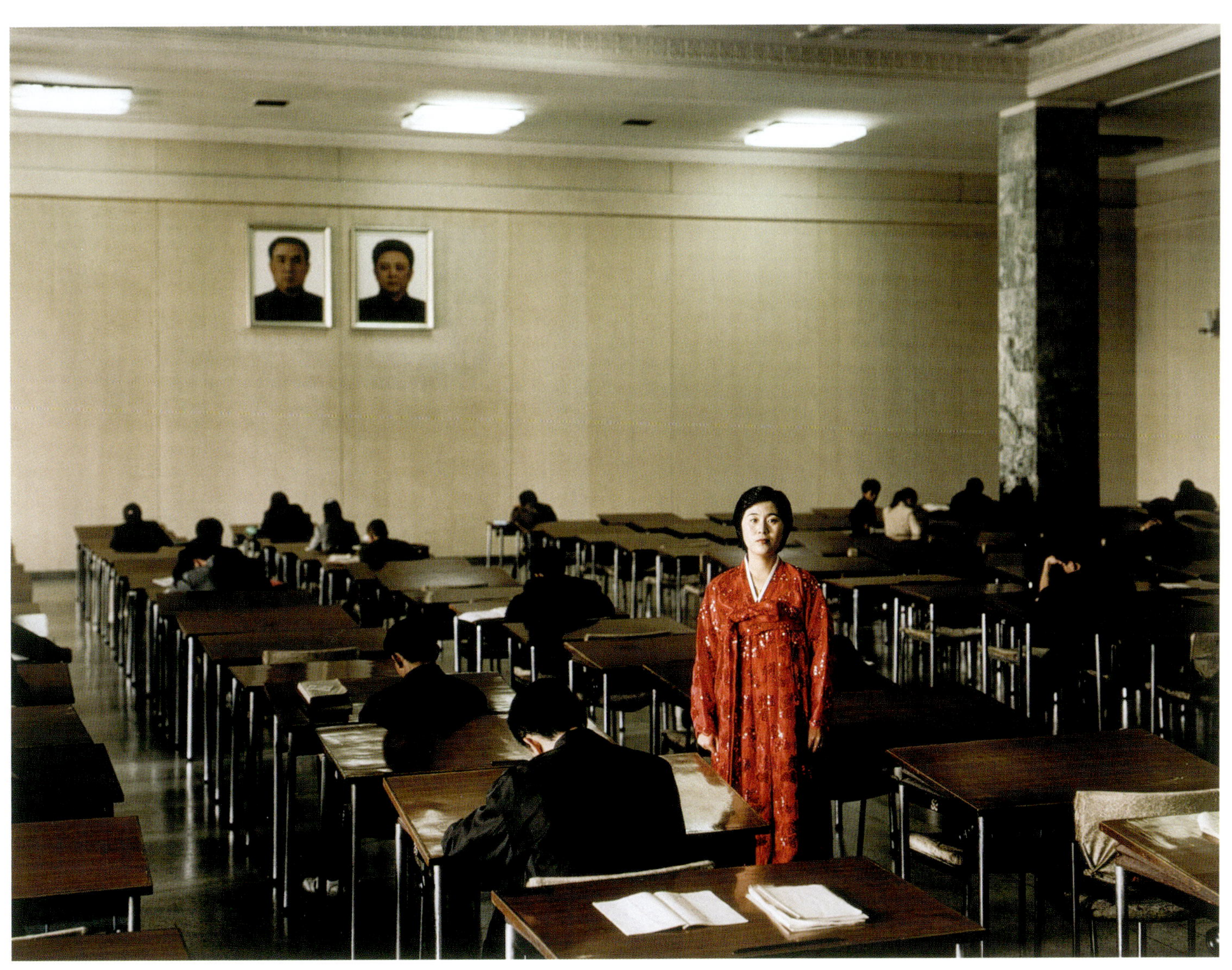

John Nassari **Girl, Dressed Up – East London**
January 2005

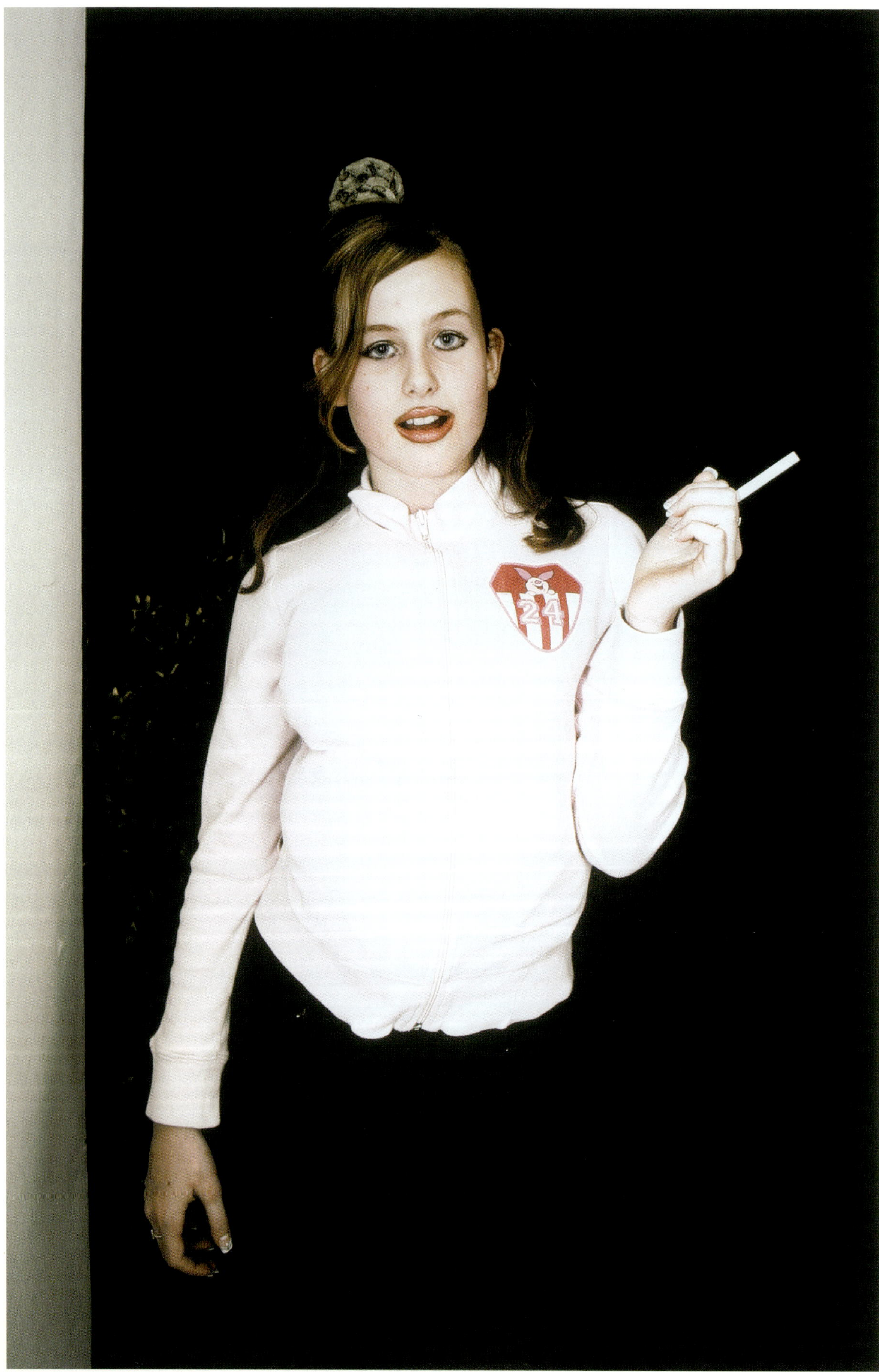

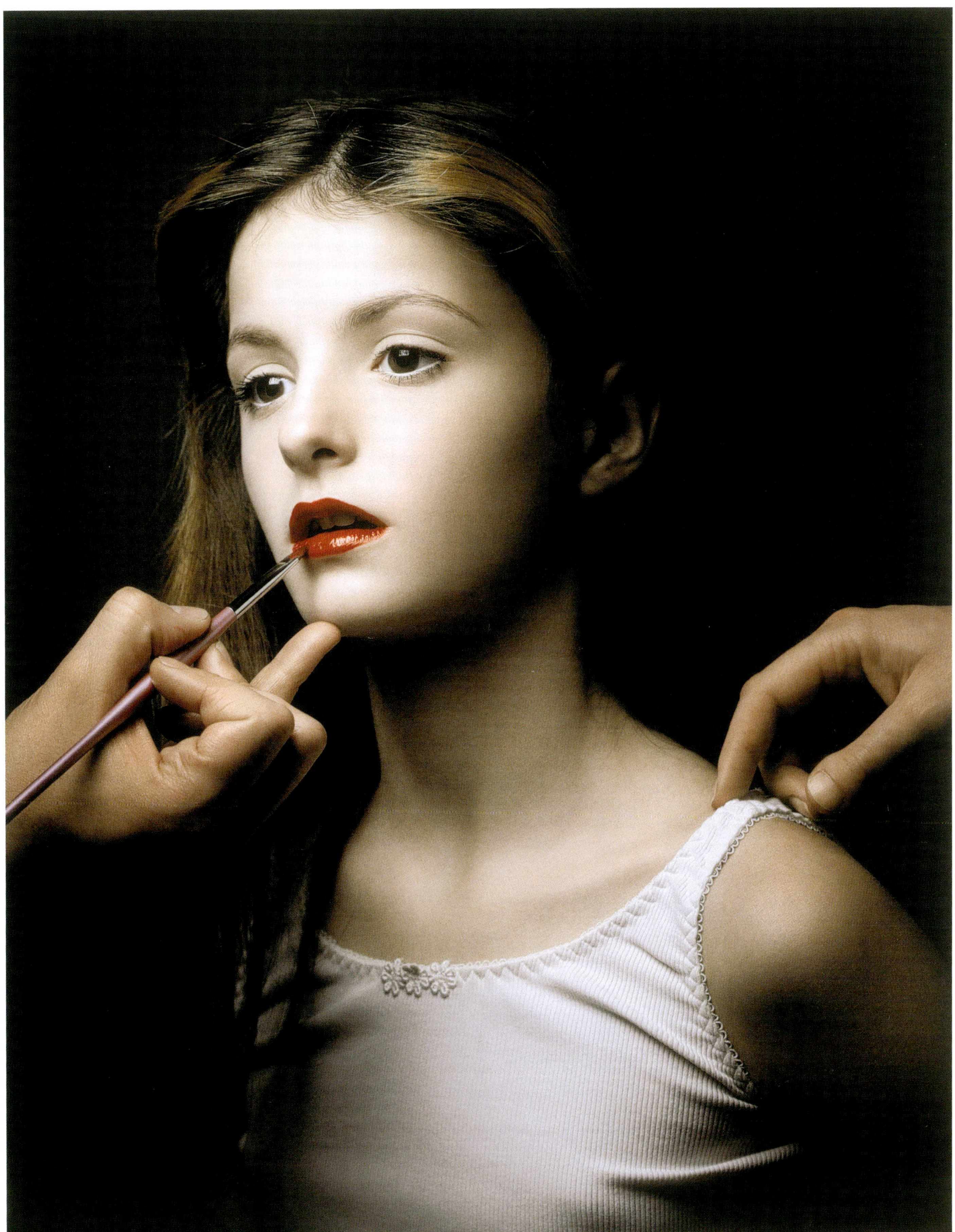

Aimée Hoving and Anoush Abrar Pinceau à la Bouche [Painting Lips] December 2005

Garth Walker   Louise – 1st Birthday
[First anniversary
of her child's birth]
January 2006

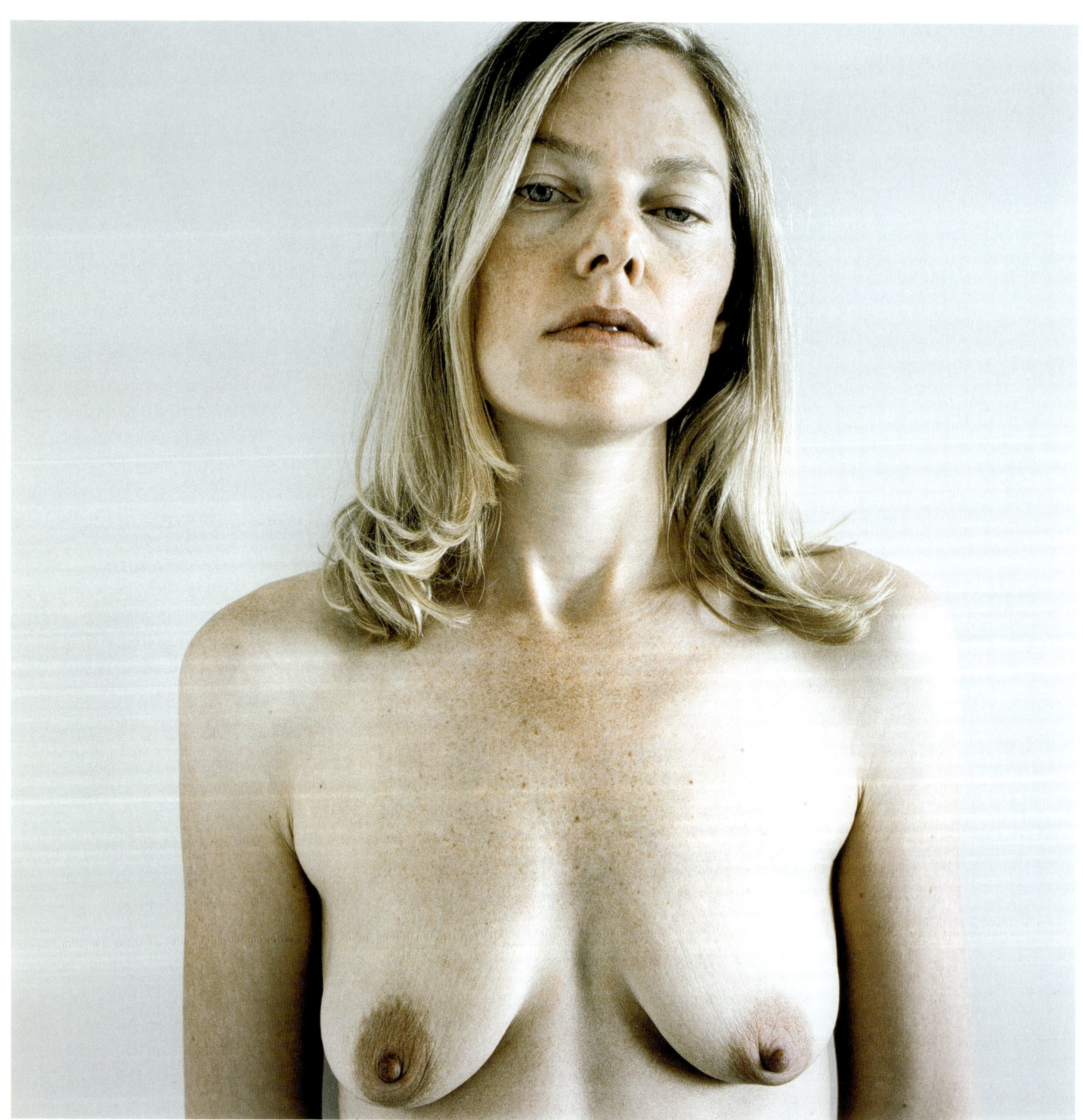

Bettina von Zwehl

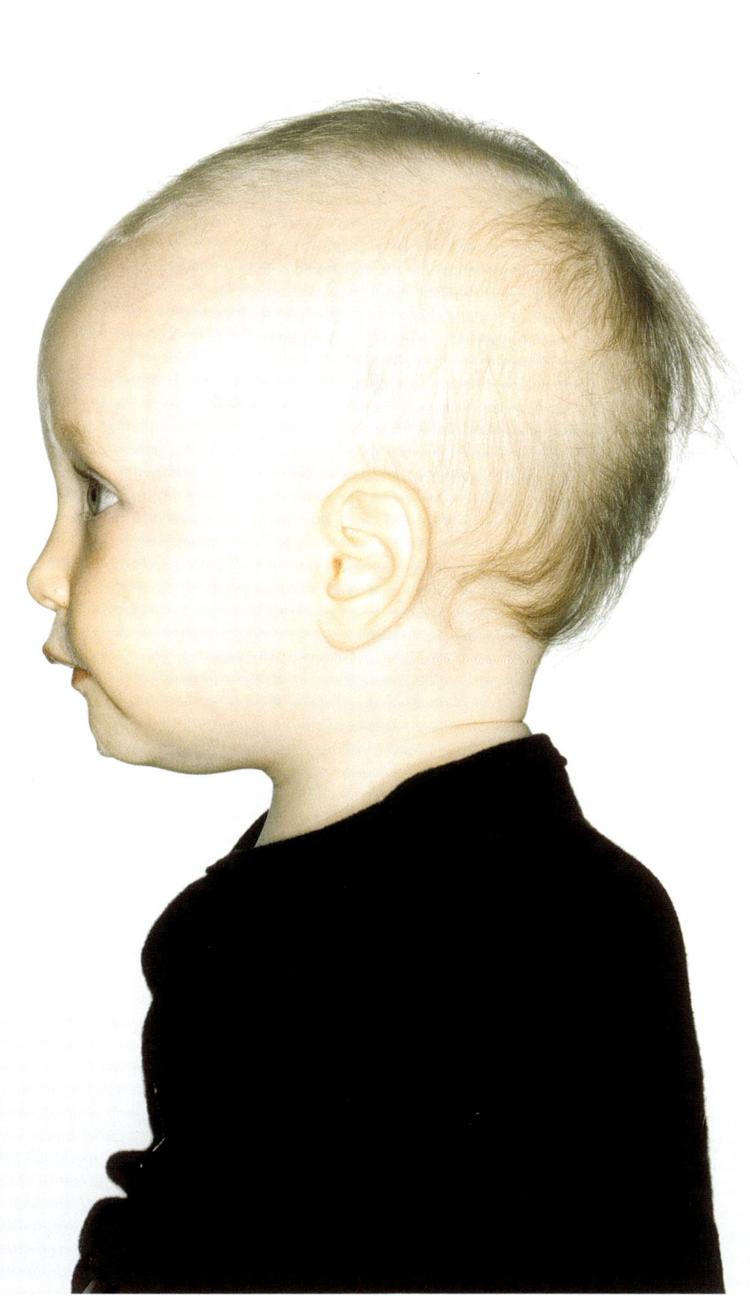

Jacob
Silberberg

Iraqi Man Waits
for US Marines
to Leave his
House
June 2005

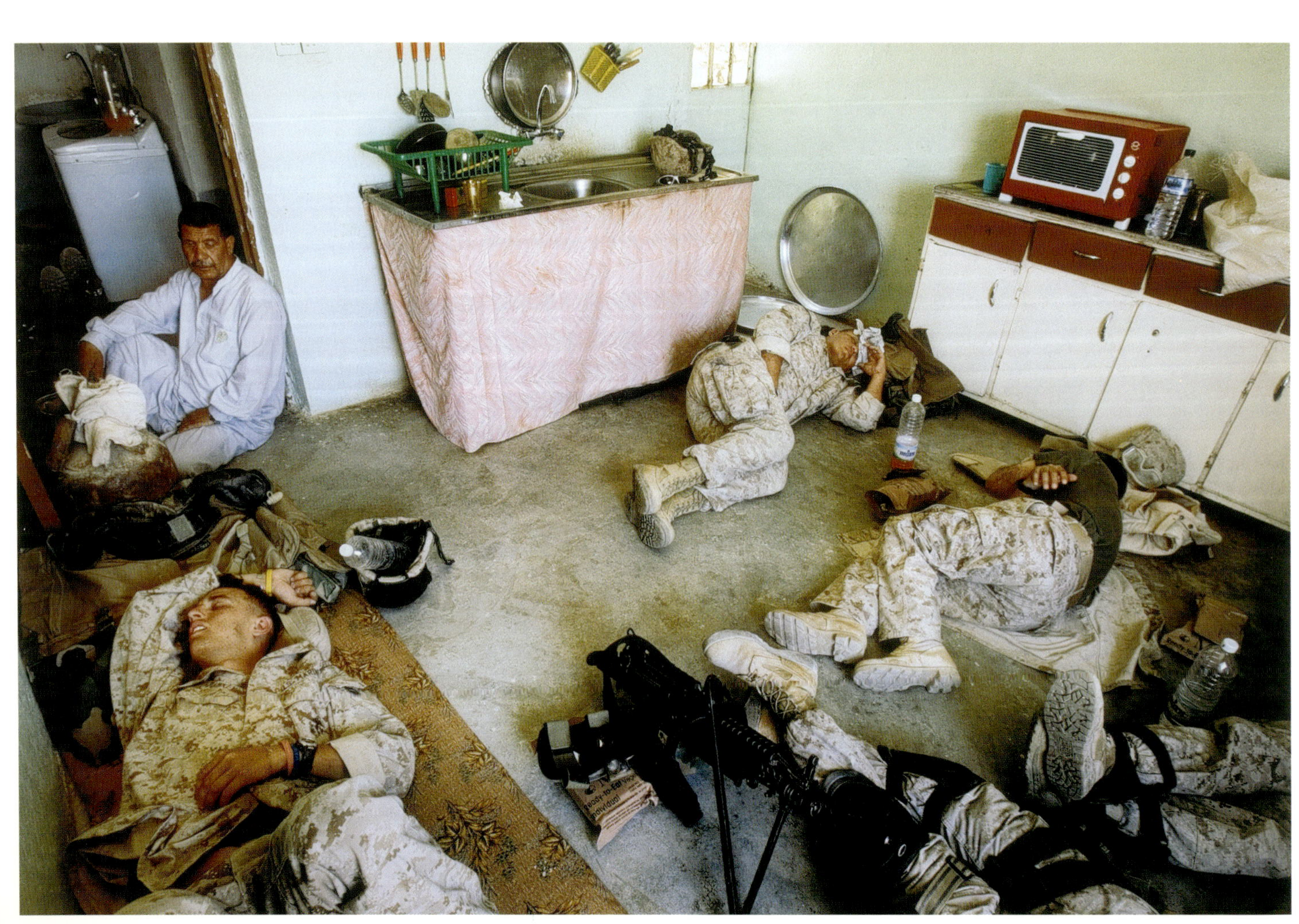

Sharad Haksar Wedding Car 3
from the series
Wedding Car
March 2005

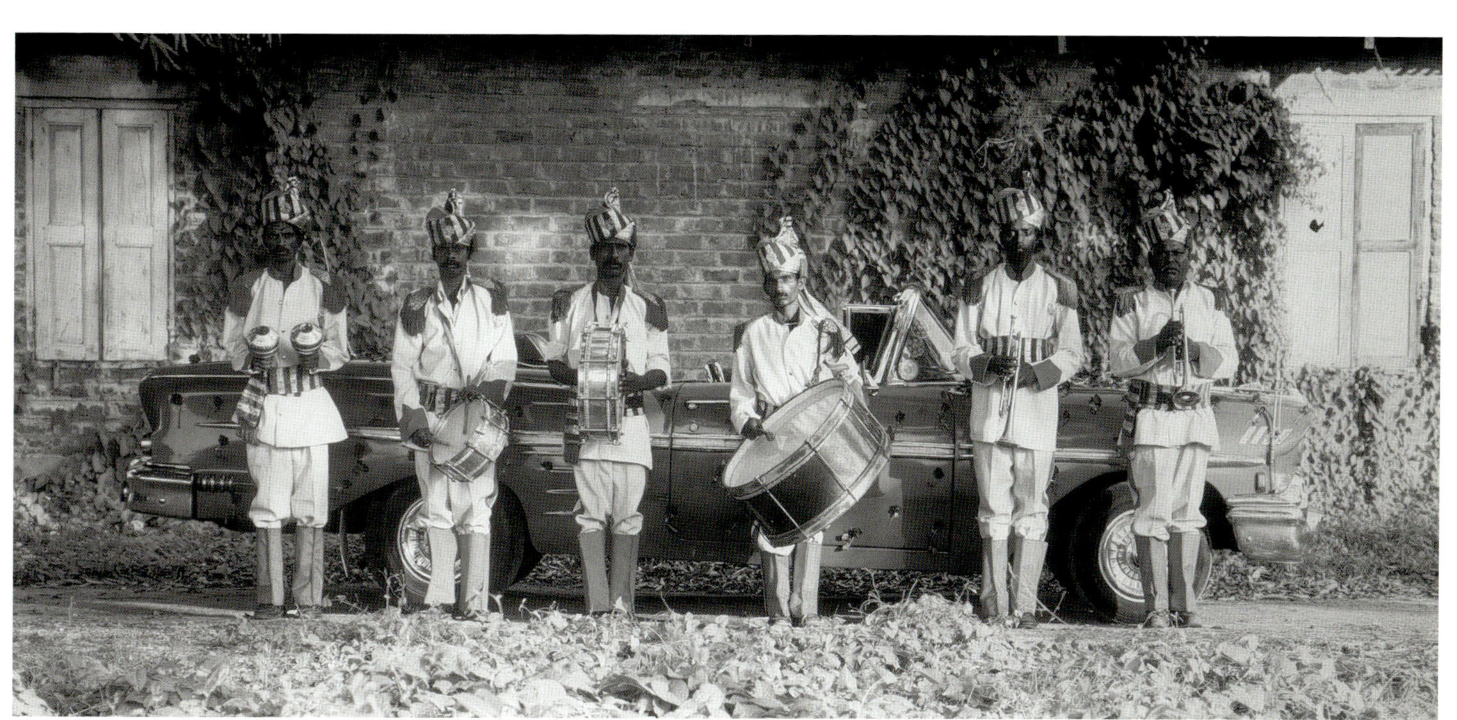

David Stewart	Mister Valentine
from the series
Relations
October 2005

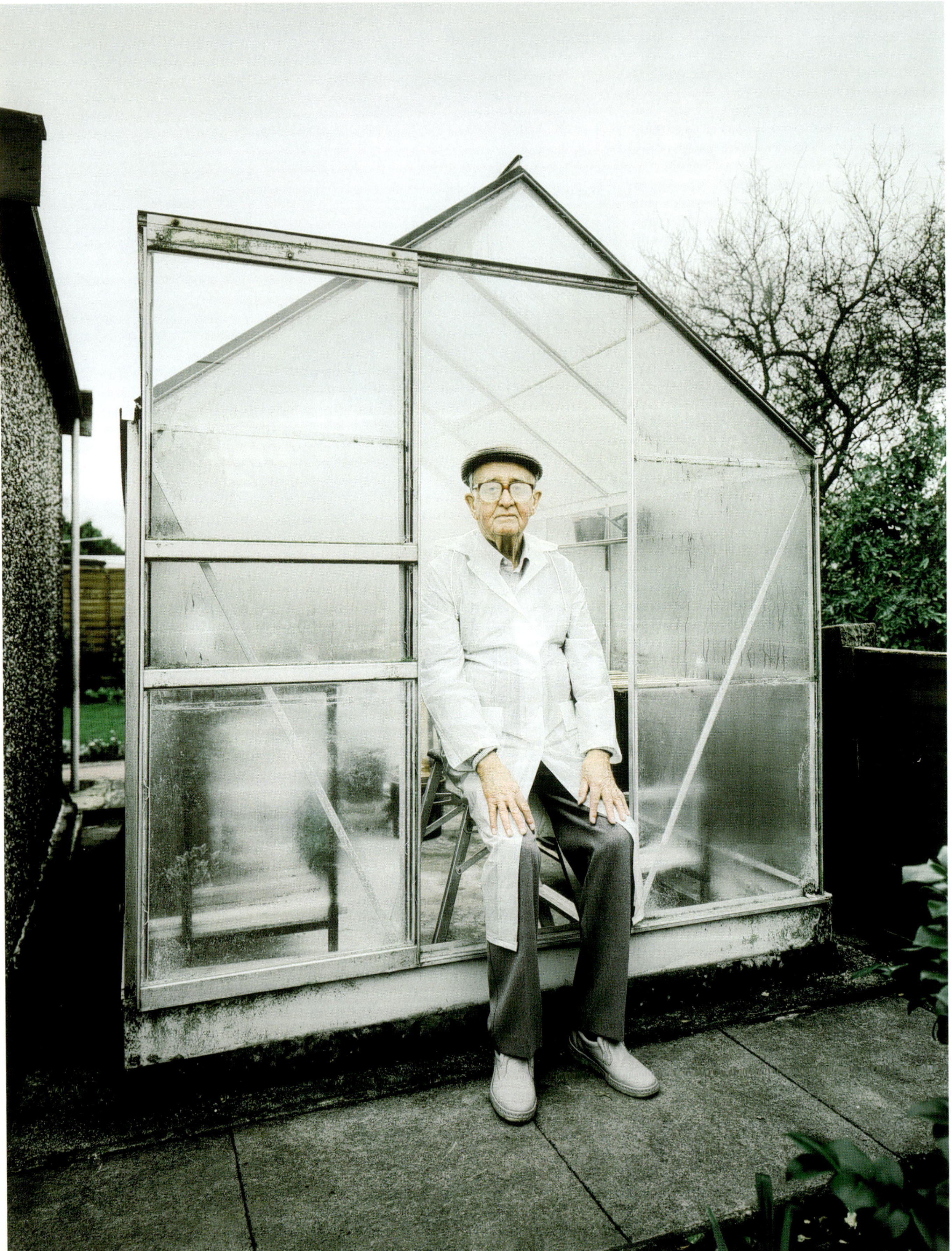

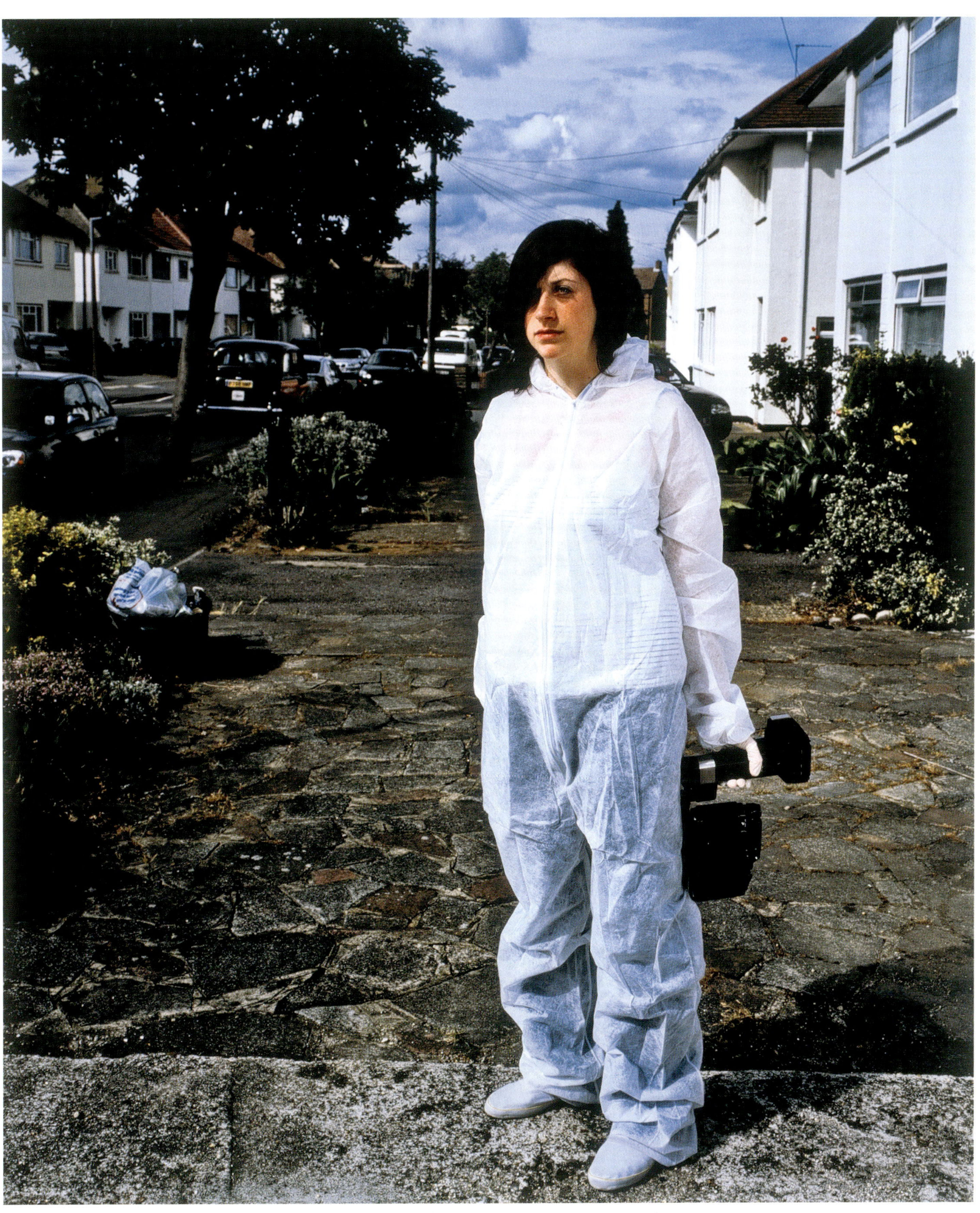

Michiru Nakayama **Father and Daughter with Violins** *from the series* **English Box** February 2006

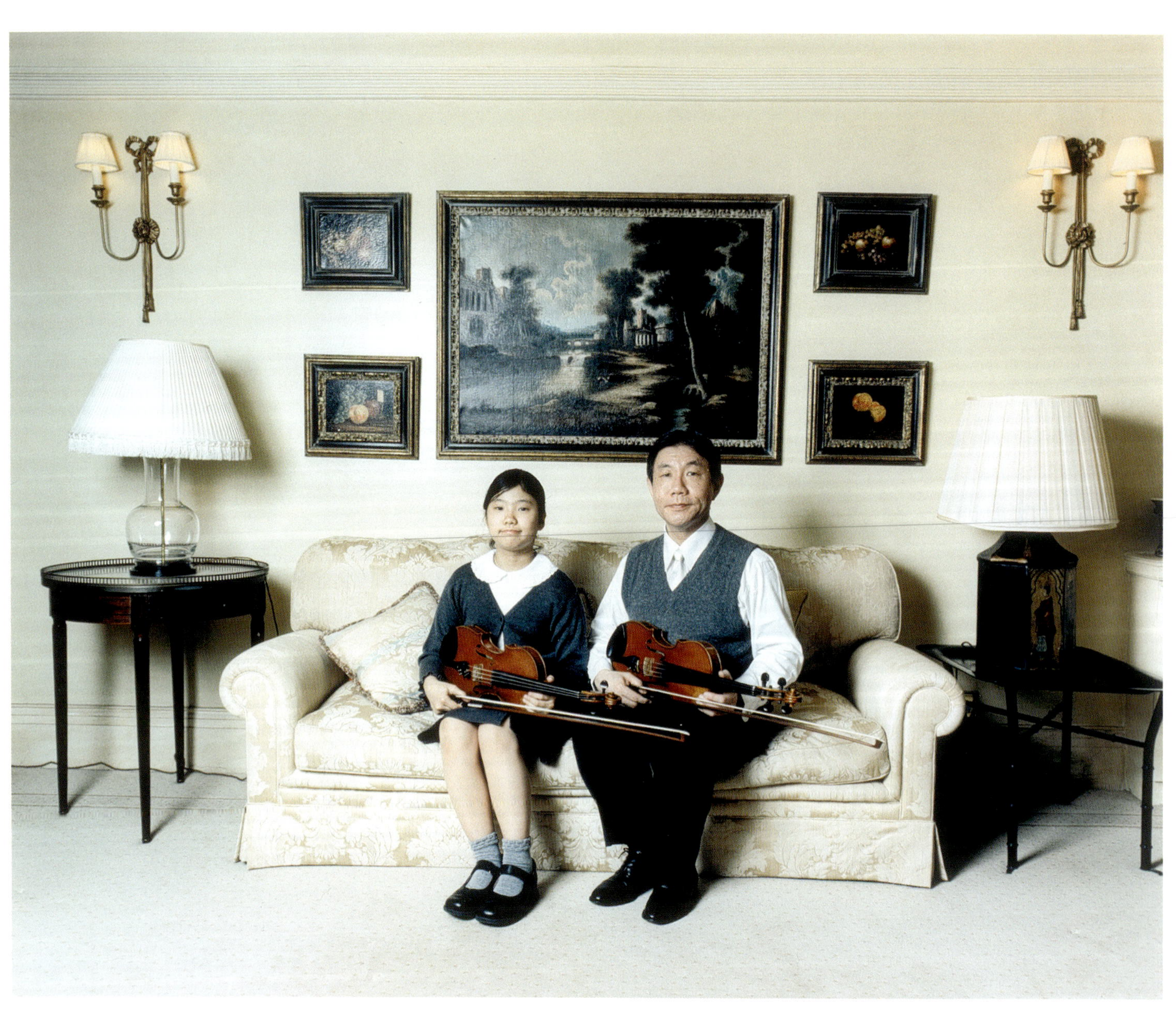

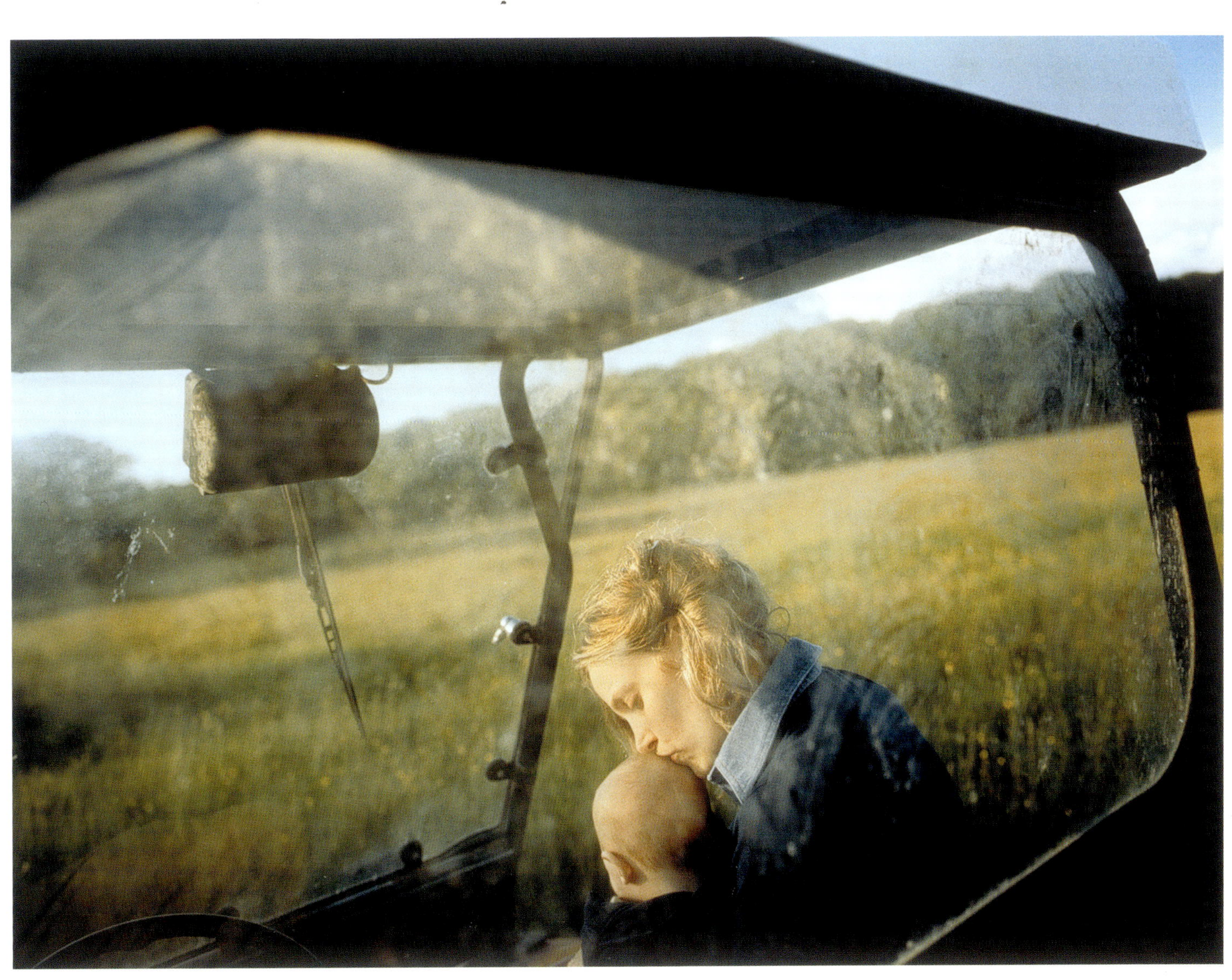

Alex ten Napel Hilde
from the series
Water Portraits
March 2006

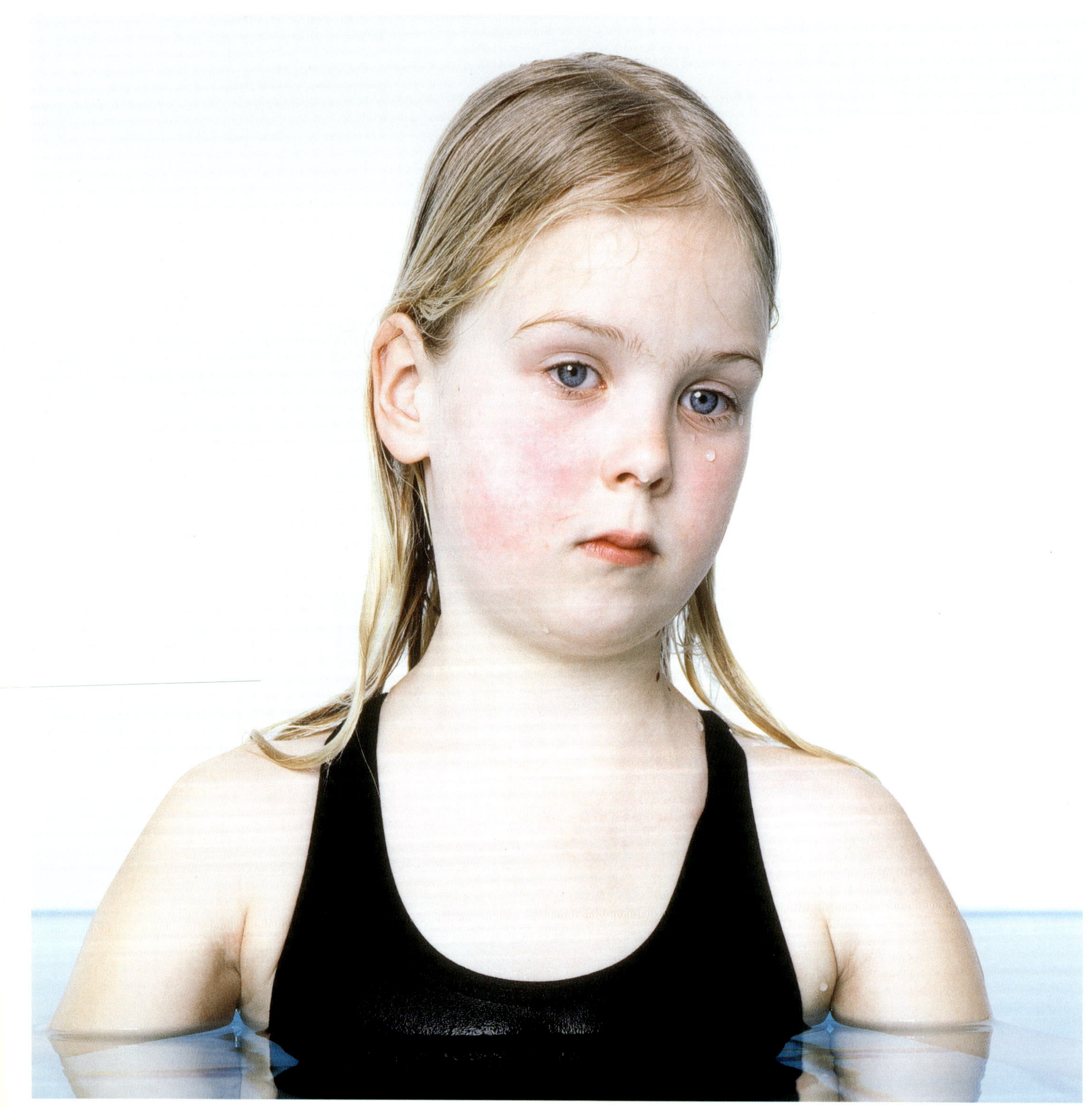

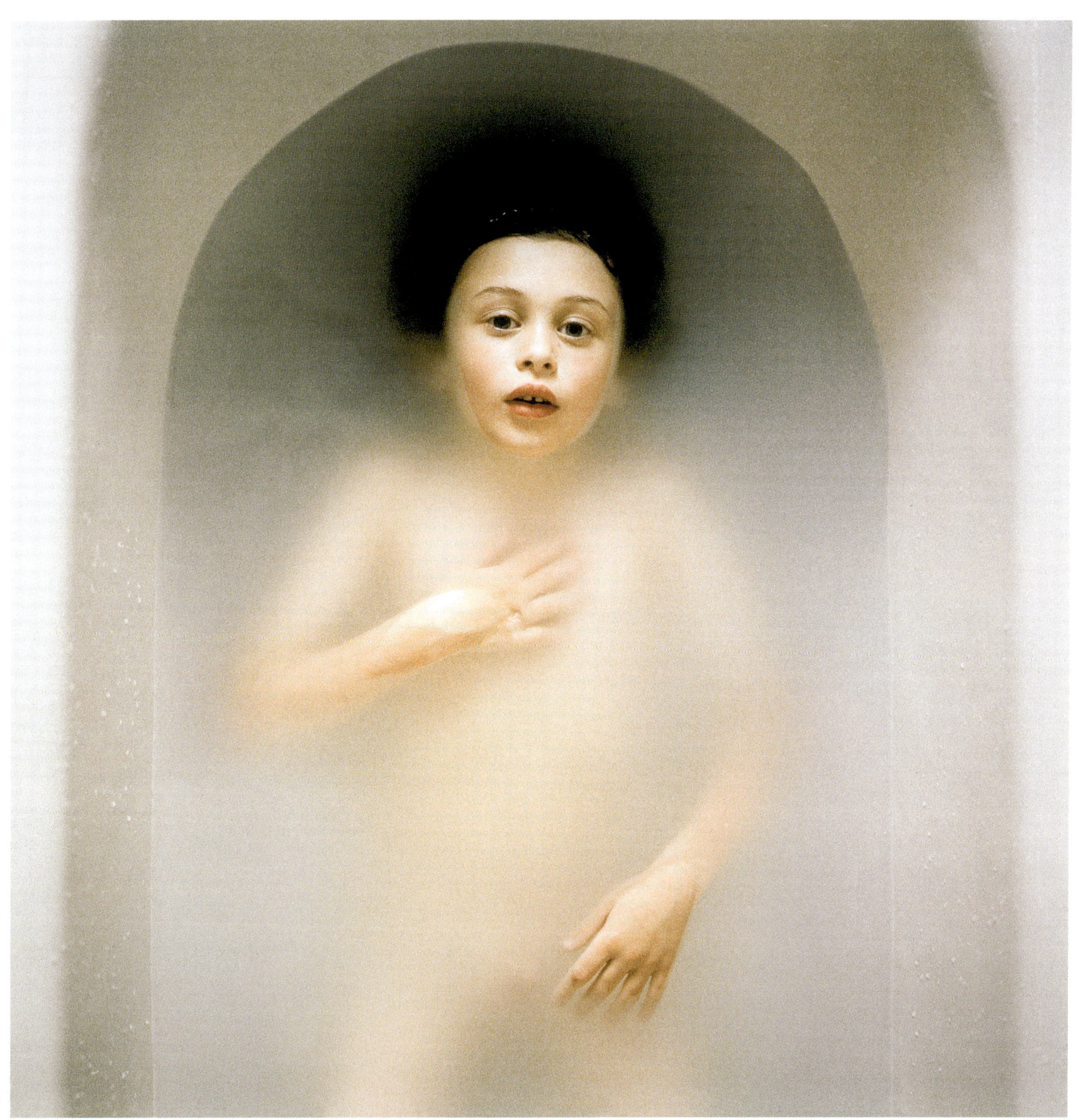

Venetia
Dearden

Charlene in her
Caravan
from the series
Somerset
August 2005

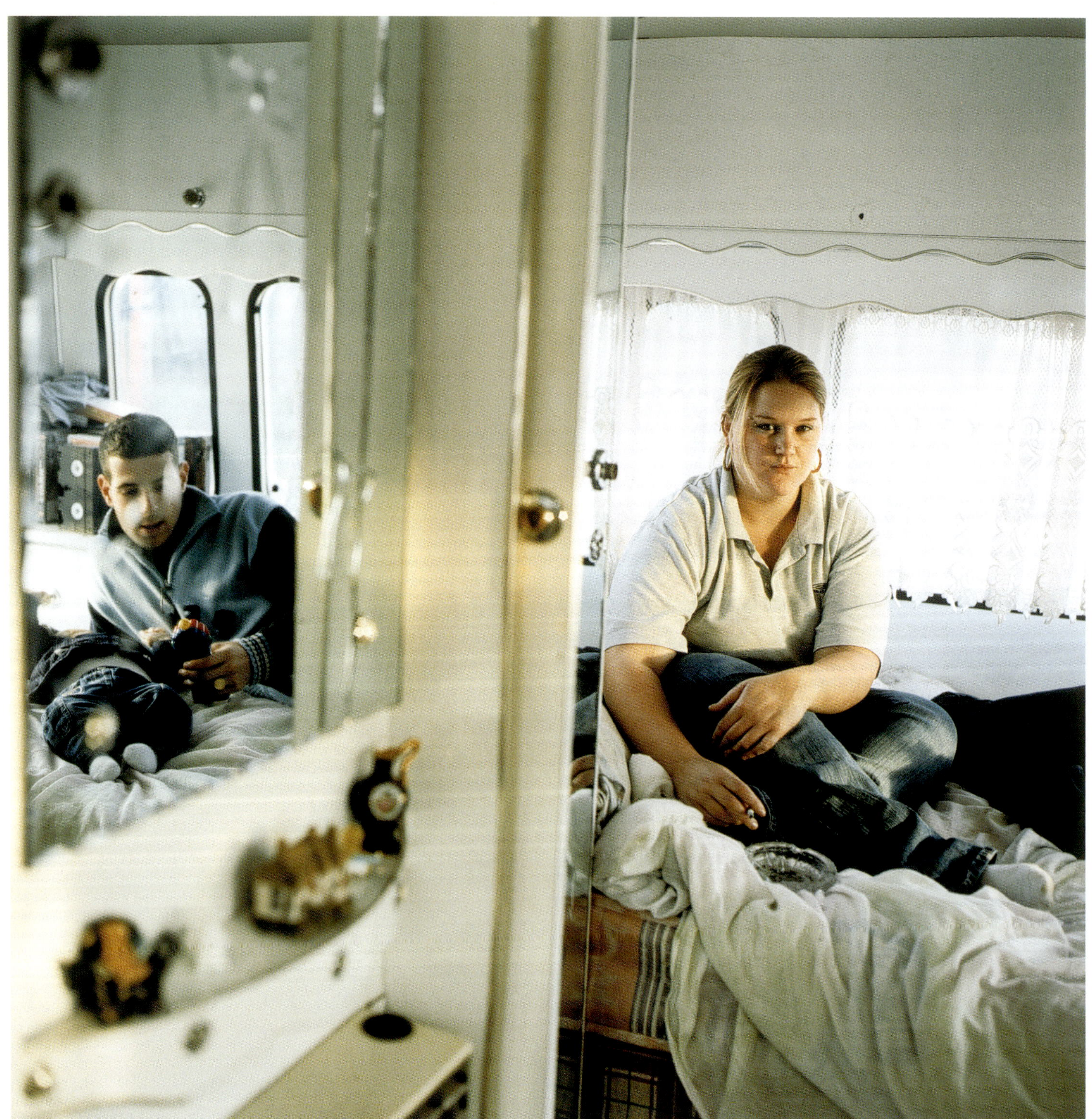

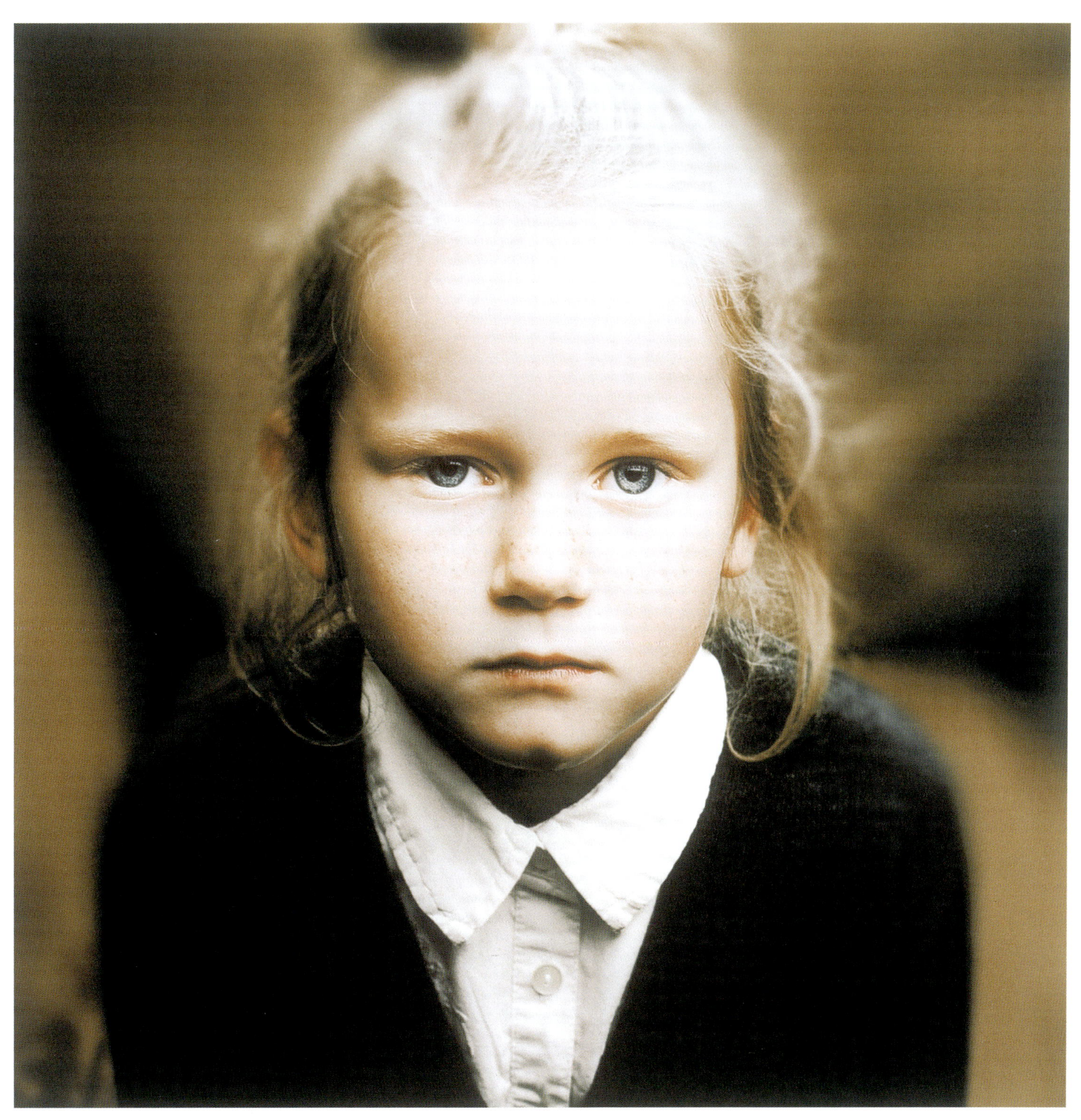

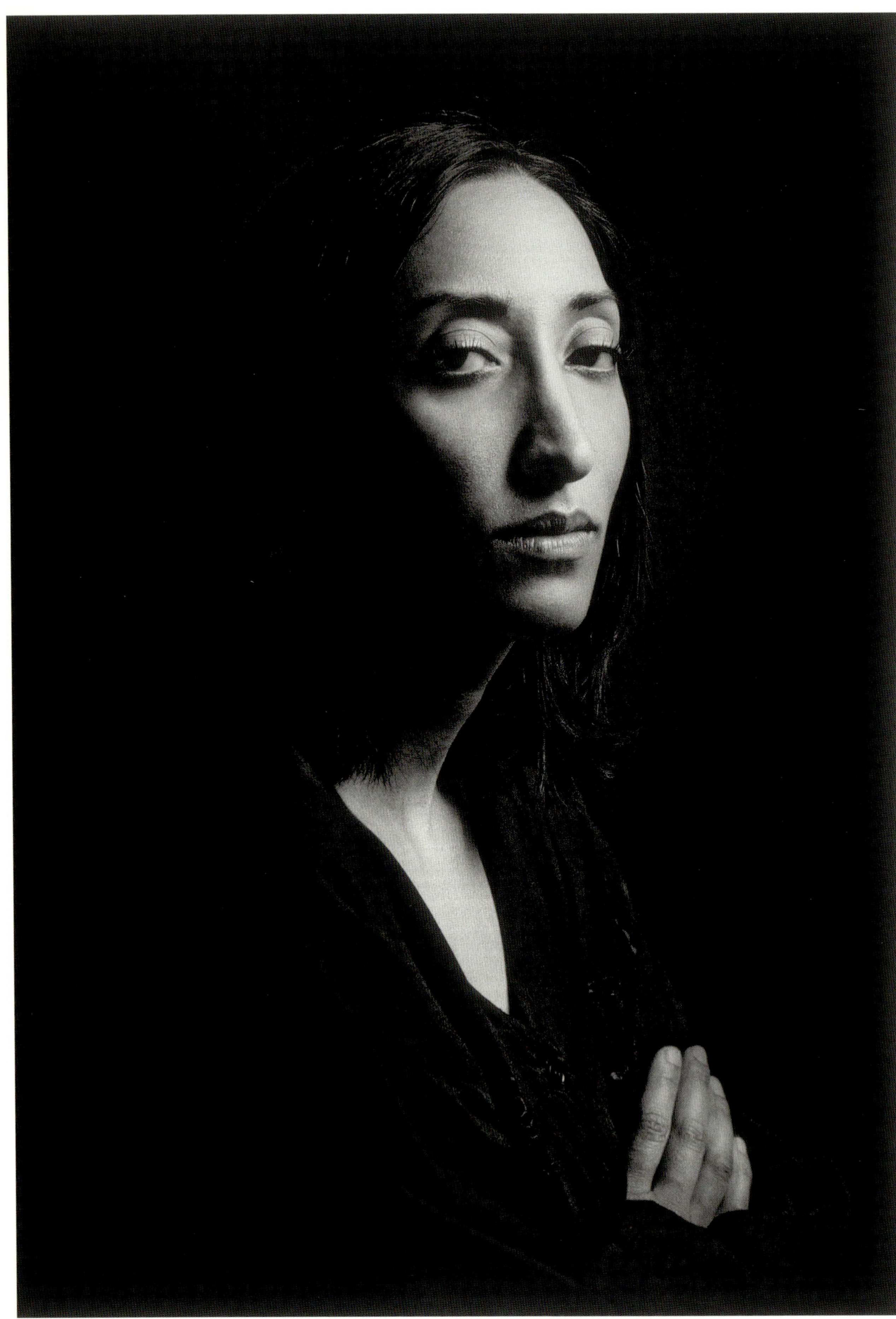

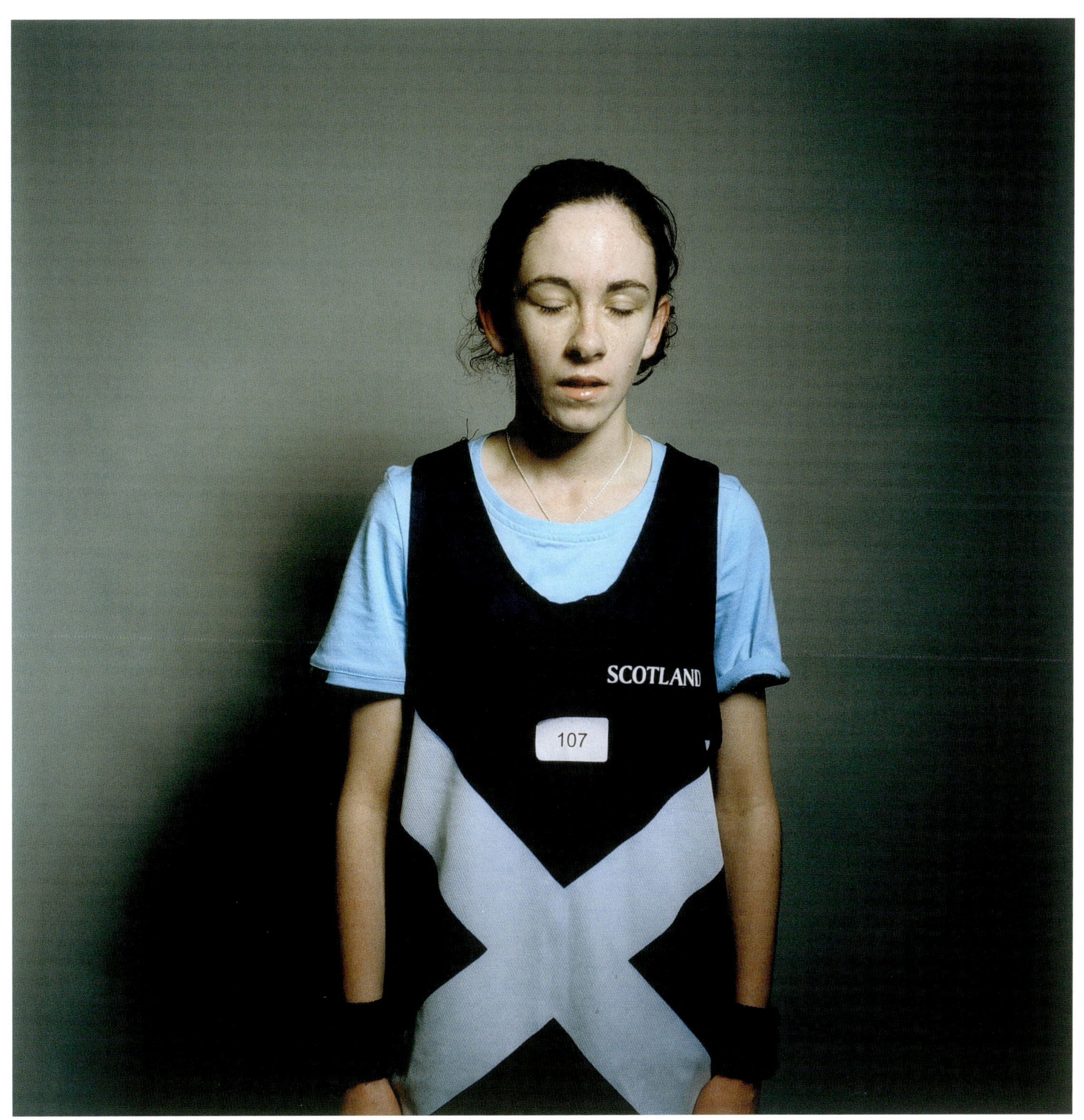
SCOTLAND
107

**Tomoko
Suwa-Krüll**

**David Bailey,
December 12th
2005**
December 2005

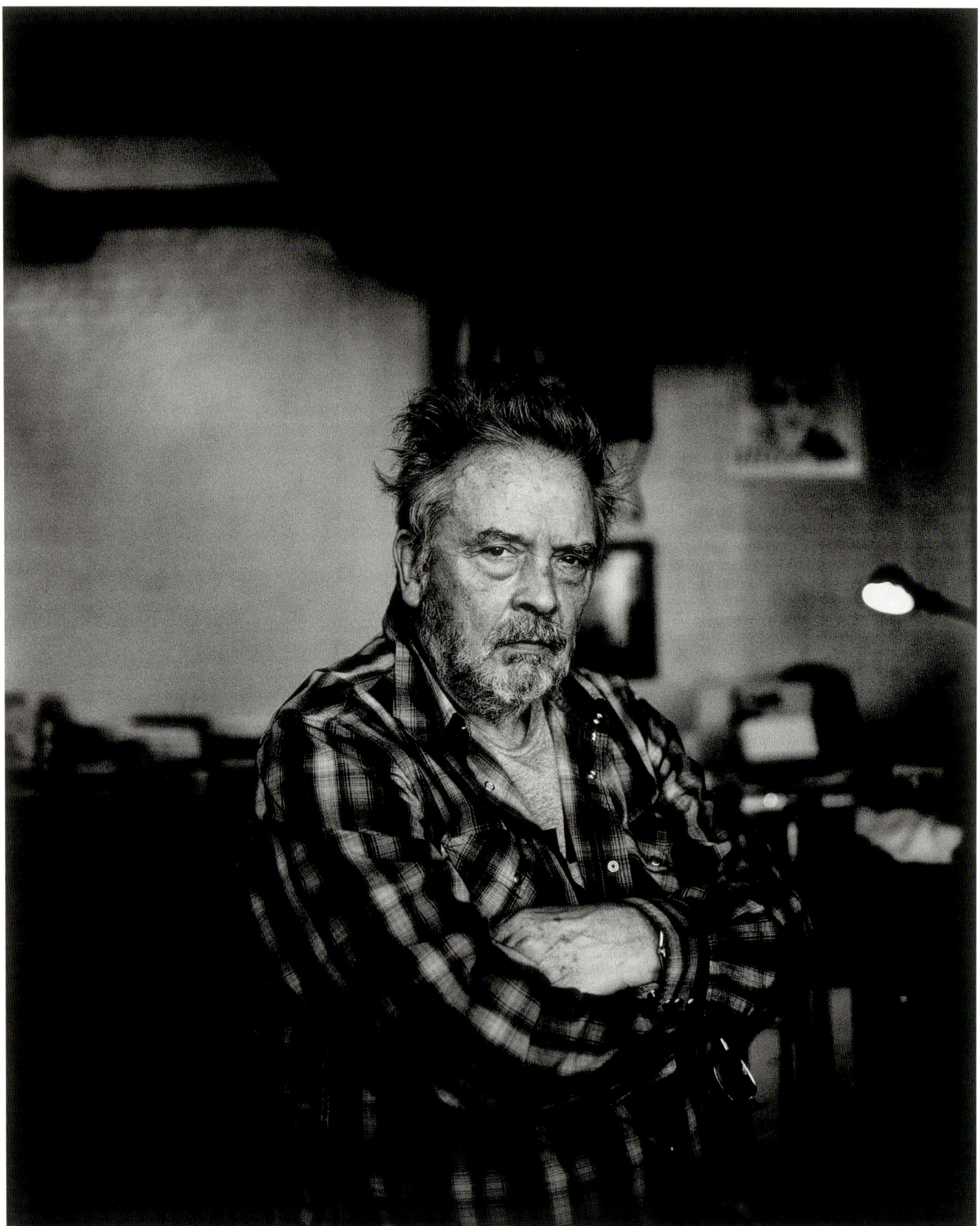

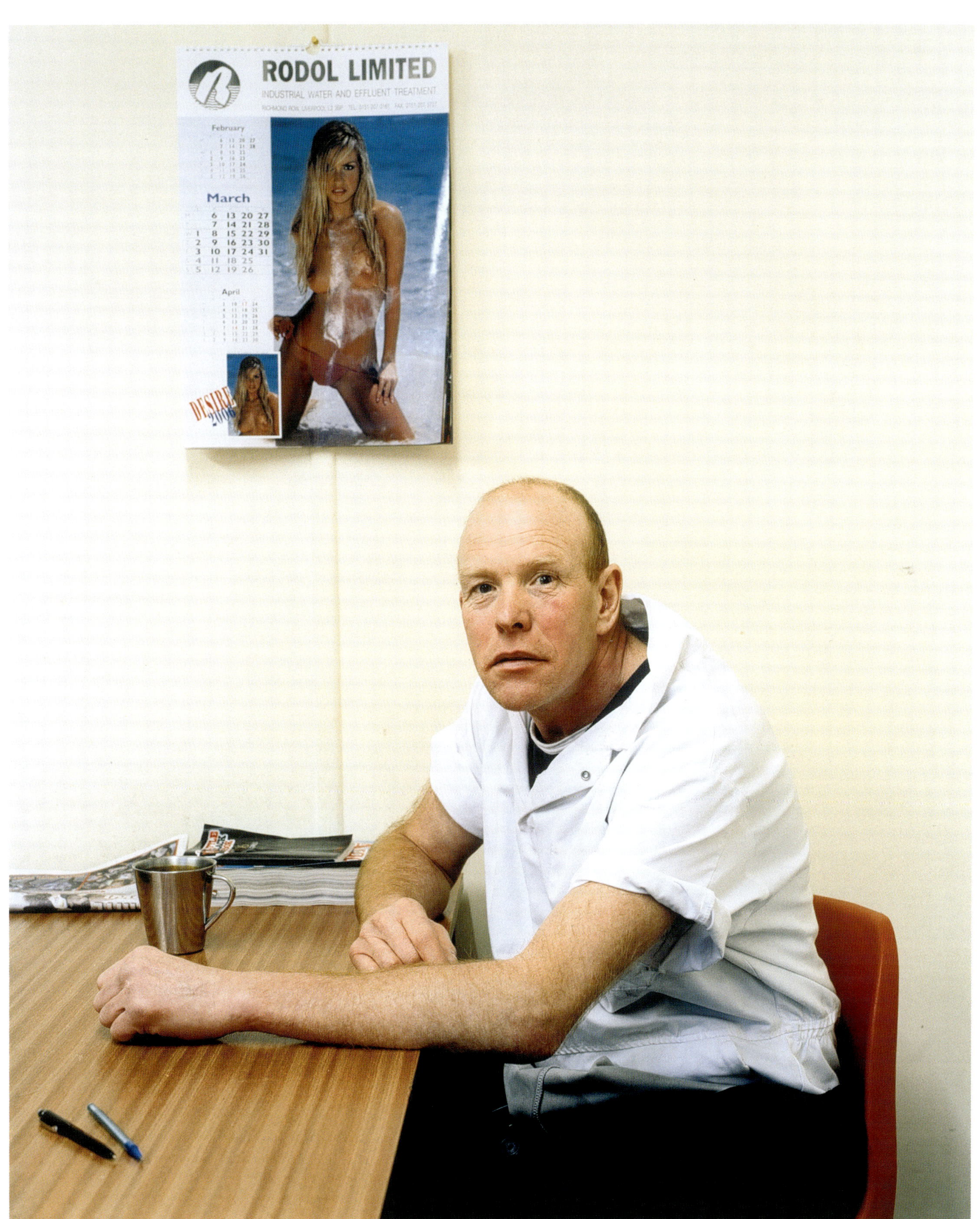
RODOL LIMITED
INDUSTRIAL WATER AND EFFLUENT TREATMENT
February
March
April
DESIRE 2006

John Ferguson **Michael
Jackson**
May 2006

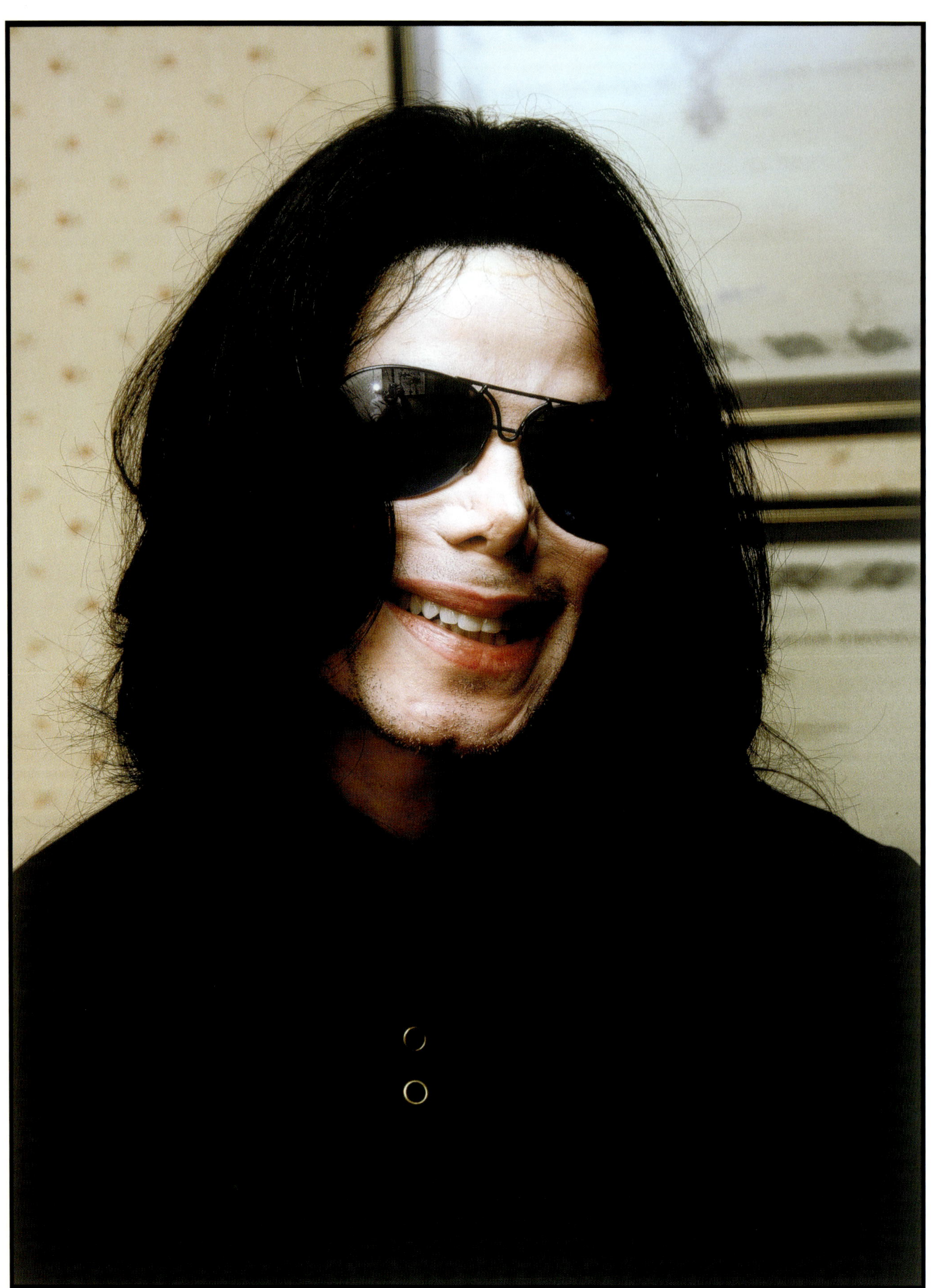

John Ferguson **Michael
Jackson**
May 2006

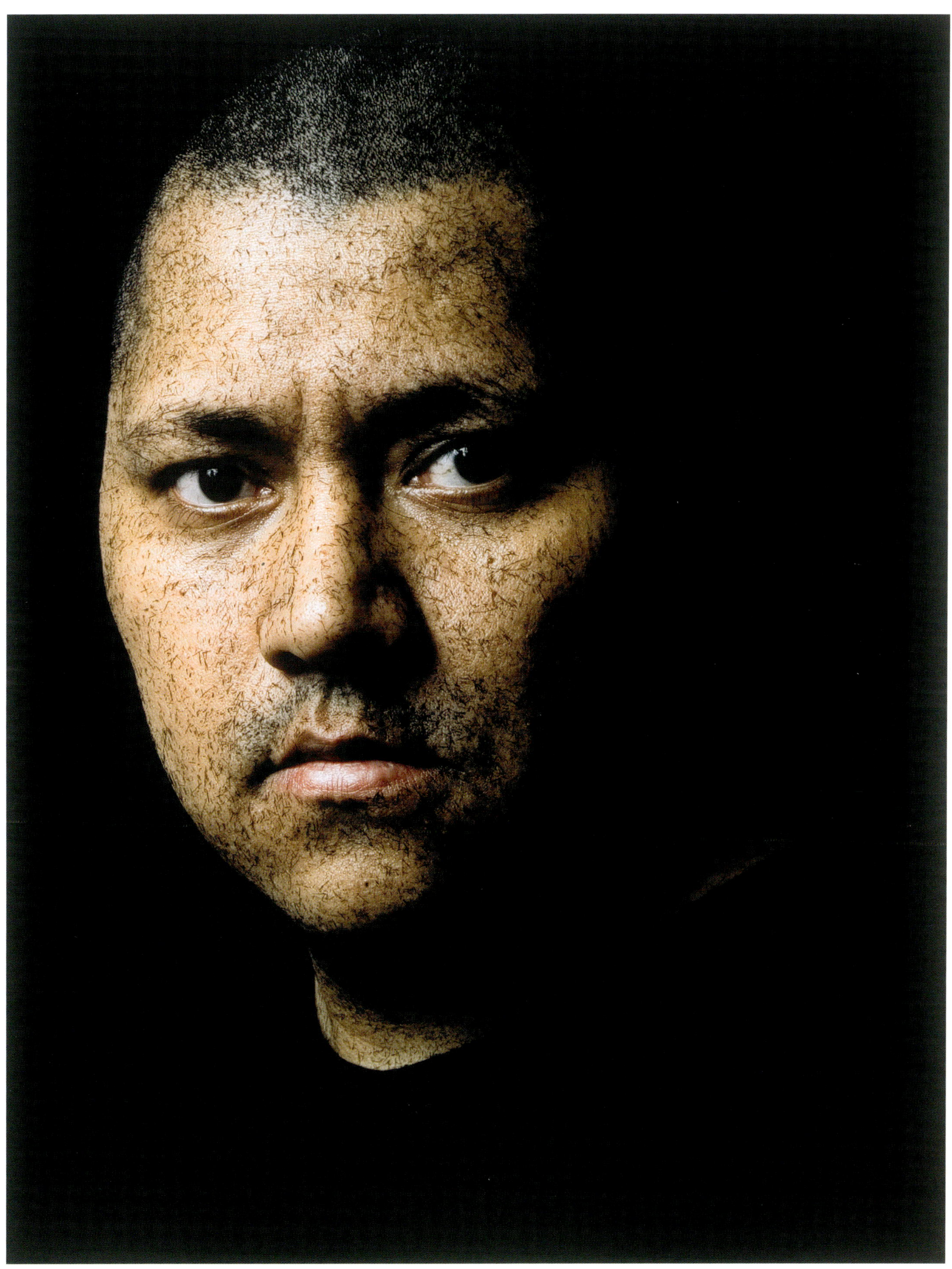

Luigi Gariglio Matilda dalla
Torre
from the series
Just Born!
April 2006

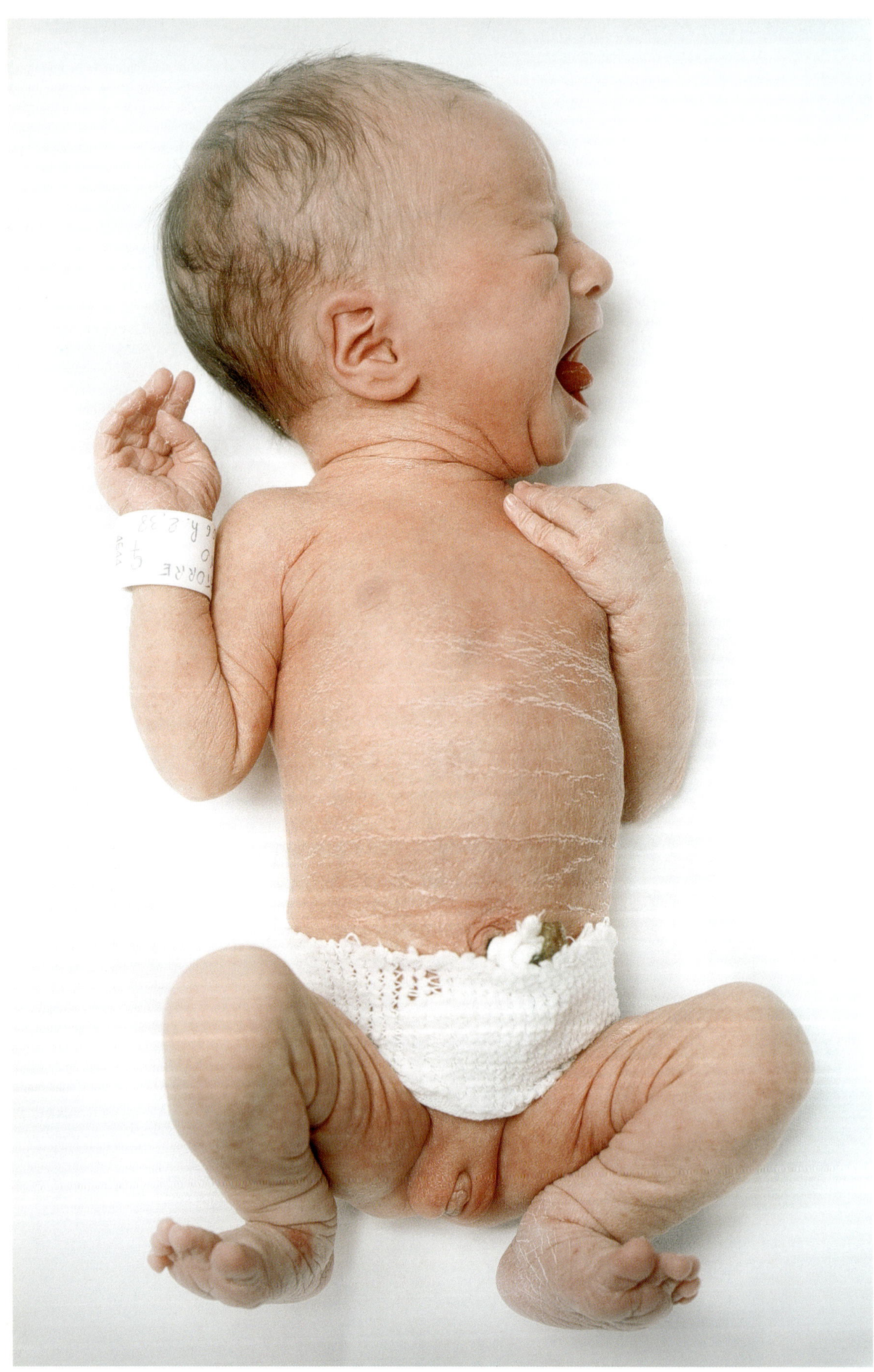

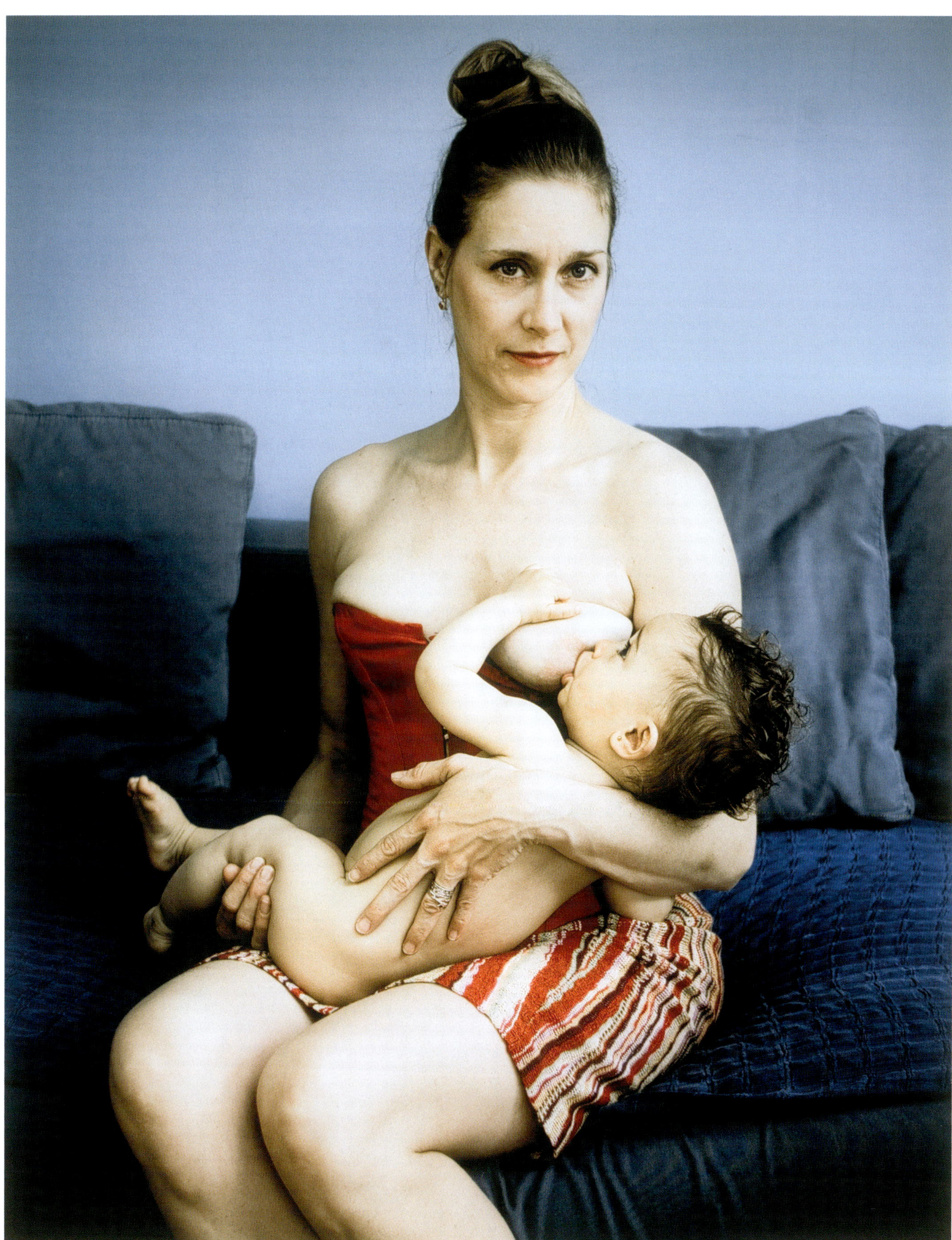

Kenneth
Griffiths

Grace and
Thurston
June 2006

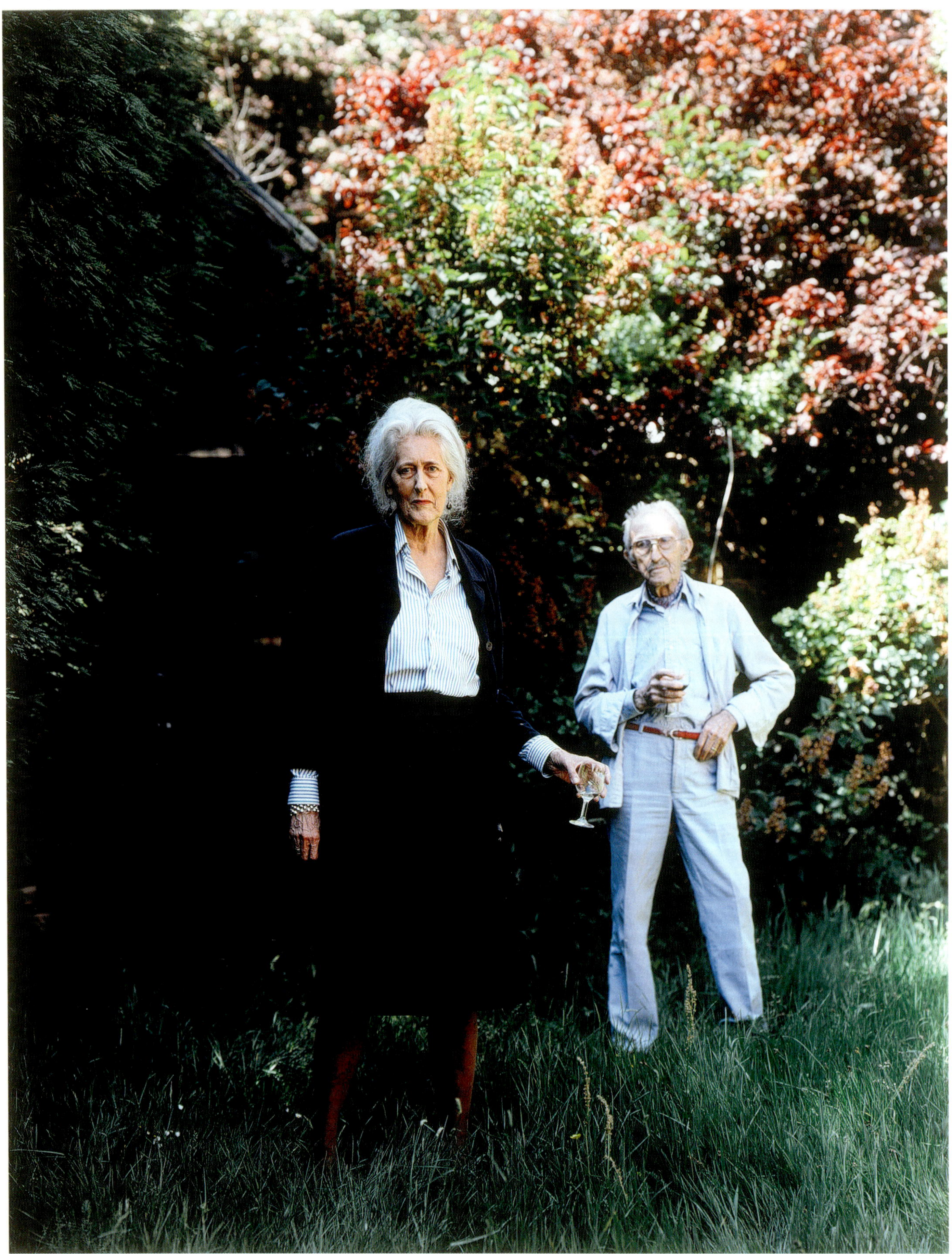

Peter
Mackertich

The 3 Sisters
from the series
Muslim Wedding
April 2005

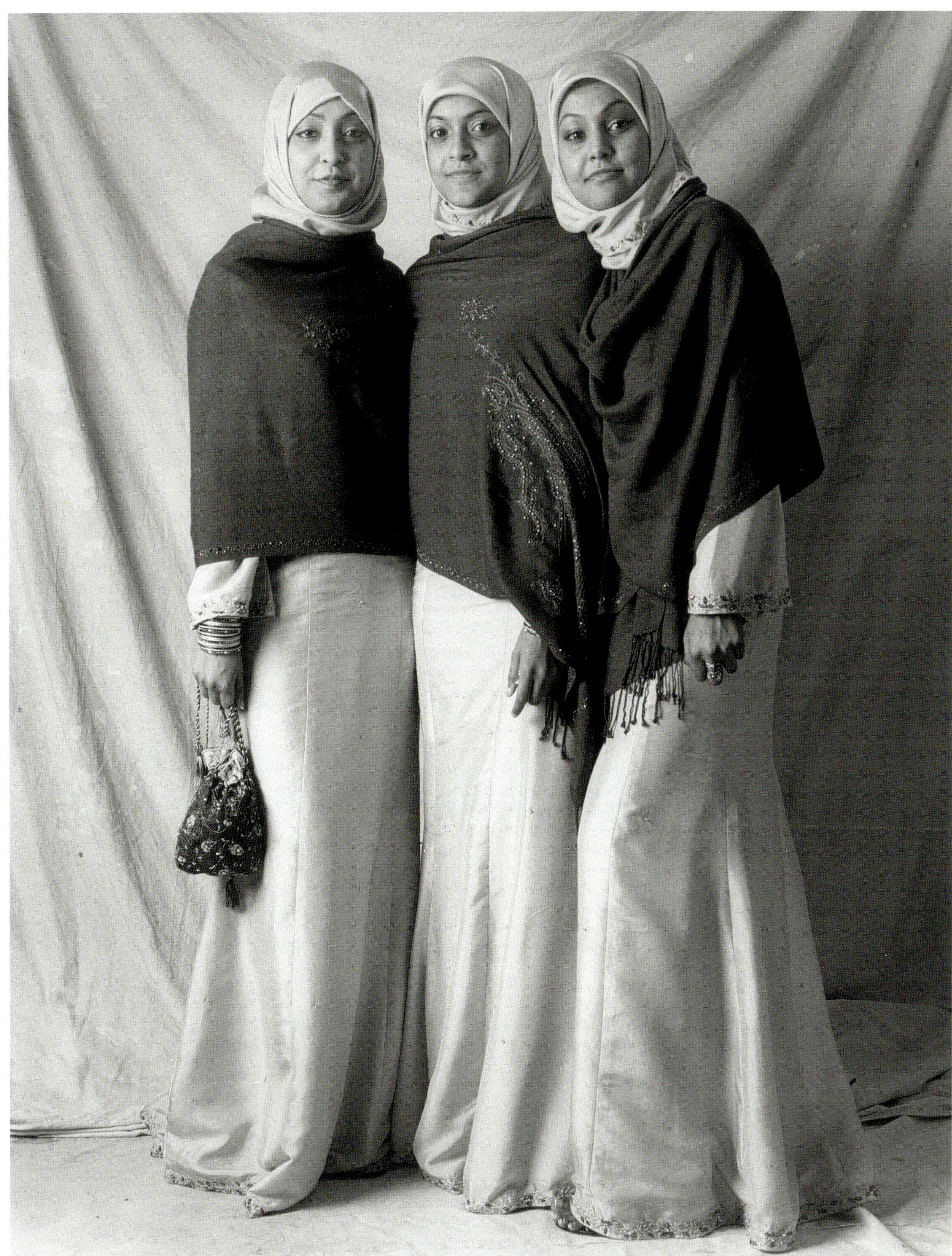

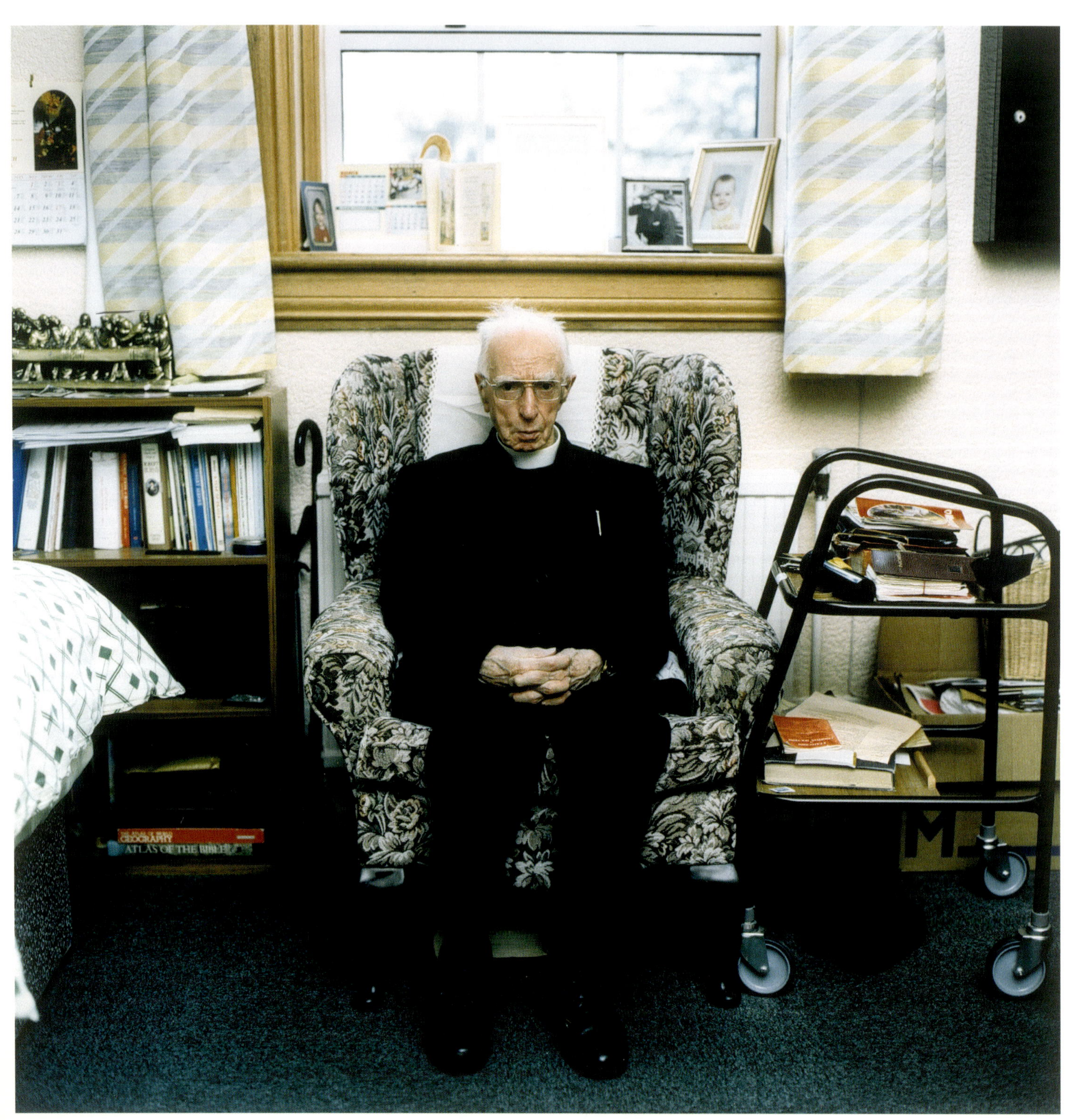

Paul Brooking   Margaret Goddard,
Librarian
July 2006

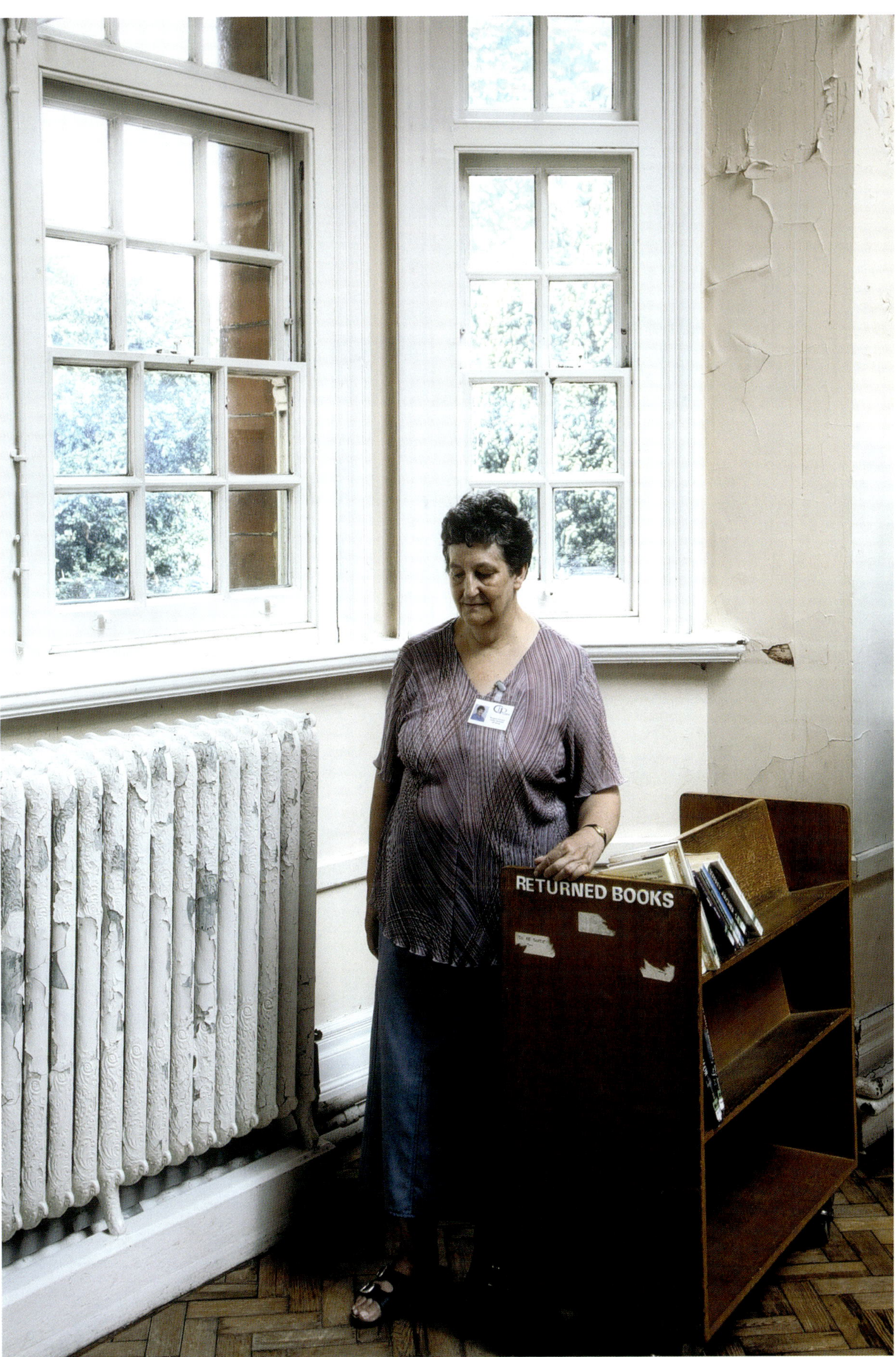

Giles Godwin Buttoning Up
from the series
Cyril
March 2006

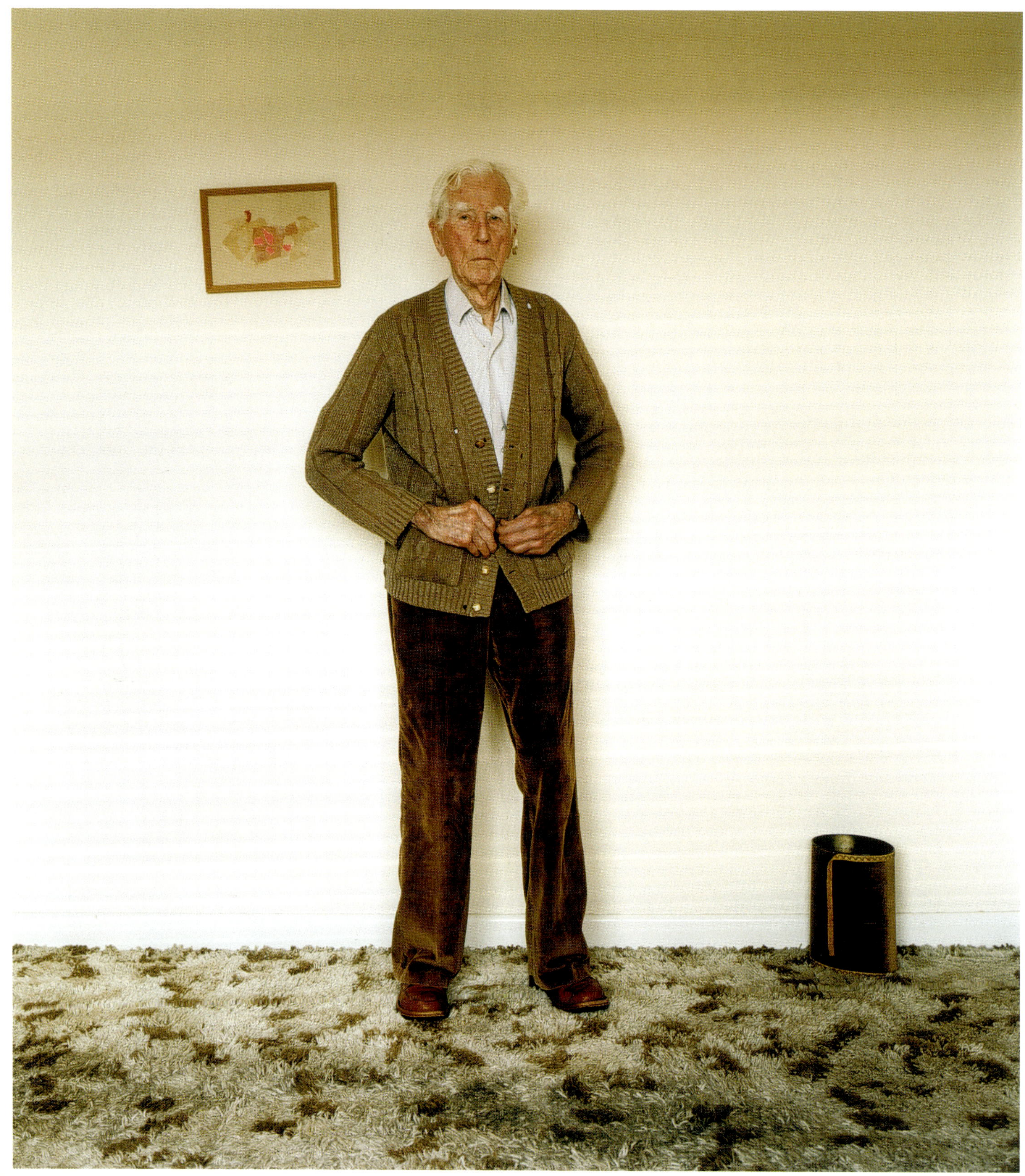

Jackie Nickerson **Sister Patrice**
from the series
Faith
March 2005

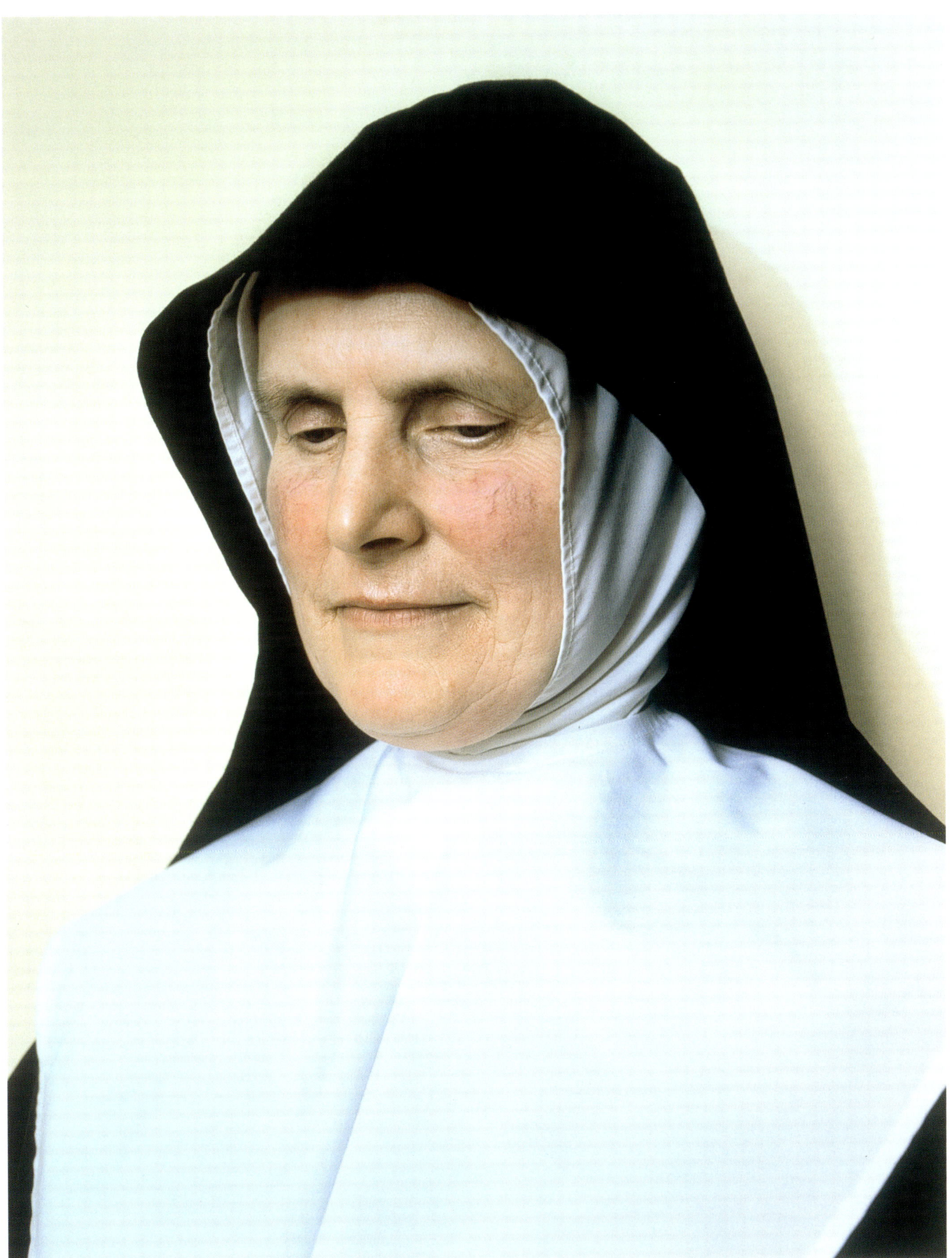

David
Simmonds

Notting Hill
Carnival
August 2005

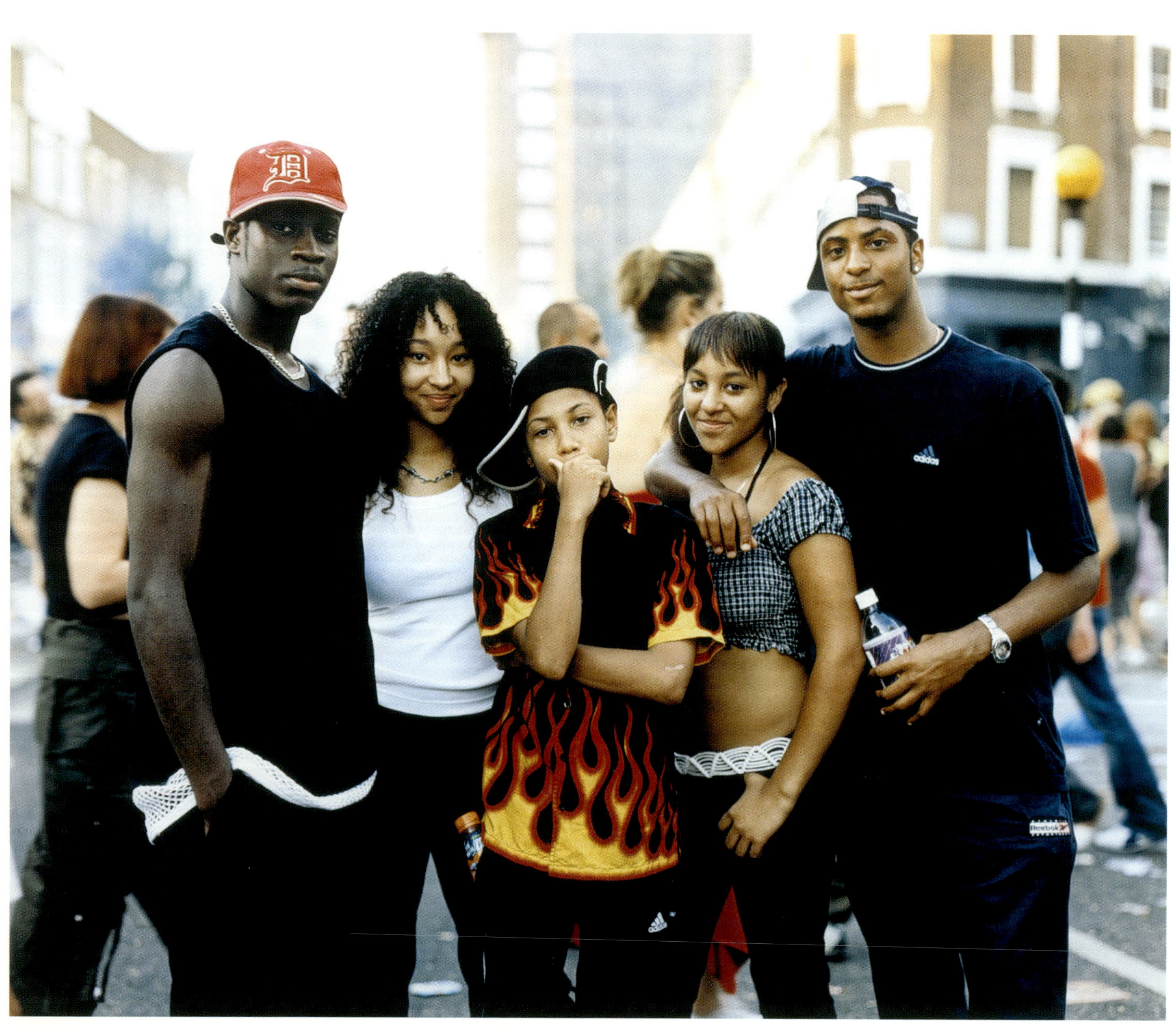

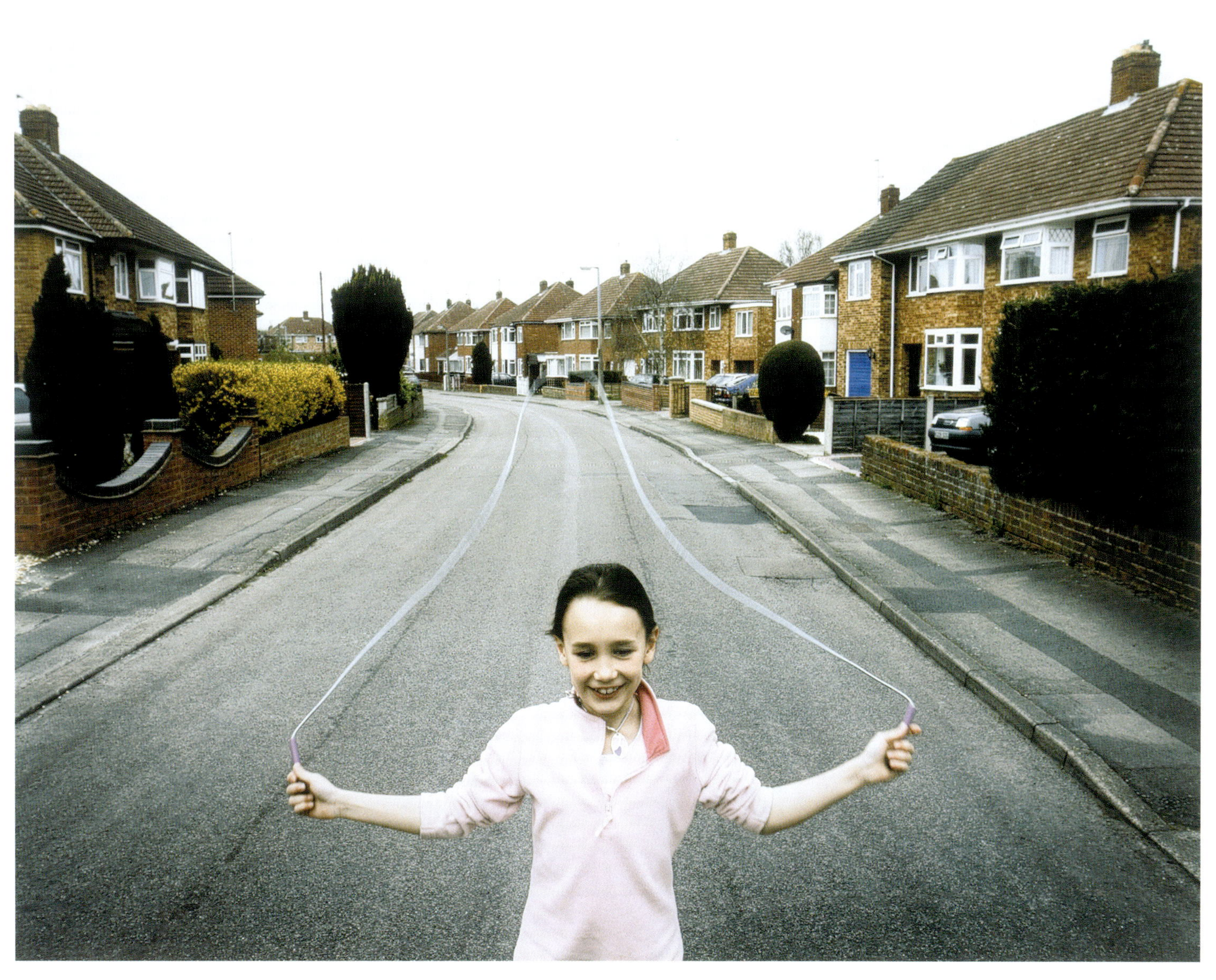

List of Exhibitors